I0698568

Unpossessable

The Surprising Key to a Sustainable Future

Roberto Siagri

Original Title: La Servitizzazione – dal Prodotto al Servizio per un Futuro Sostenibile senza Limiti alla Crescita © 2021 Guerini

Author: Roberto Siagri
Title: Unpossessable: The Surprising Key to a Sustainable Future

First edition
Independently published

Copyright © 2023 by Roberto Siagri
All rights reserved.

ISBN: 9798873897964

This book may not be reproduced or transmitted in any form without the written permission of the author. Every effort has been made to make this book as accurate as possible. Although the author and editor have prepared this book with the greatest of care, and have made every effort to ensure its accuracy, we assume no responsibility or liability for errors, inaccuracies or omissions. The author does not warrant that the information contained in this book is fully complete and shall not be responsible for any errors or omissions.

*"The most important thing about Spaceship Earth
—an instruction book didn't come with it."*

Richard Buckminster Fuller

Contents

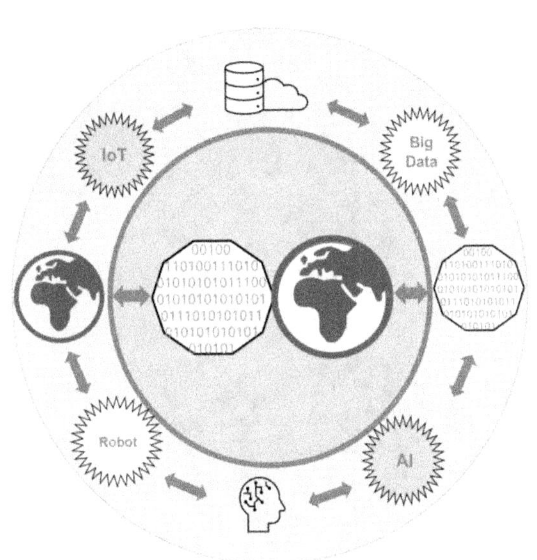

IoT
Big
Data
Robot
AI

Introduction

"We are on a spaceship; a beautiful one. It took billions of years to develop. We're not going to get another. Now, how do we make this spaceship work?"

"We now have the resources, technology and know- how to make of this world a 100% physical success."

Richard Buckminster Fuller

For many years I asked myself which was the path digital technology was pointing us to. It couldn't just be an enhancement or amplification of what we were already doing. When I looked at how digital technology had transformed the world of computing and communication, it was clear to me that this transformation would spread to all other products as well.

I have written this book to convey a message that digital technologies can help us change the world for the better. They can enable us to build a truly sustainable economy, which also means a better distribution of wealth; but this wealth will be different, more aligned with true human values.

If our aim is a better distribution of wealth, the production model must necessarily be radically changed. With a planet heading towards ten billion people by the middle of this century, the industrial production model based on ownership is no longer sustainable. With such a large population, the planet's limits are becoming apparent. For us humans, the planet is no longer boundless: we are now the astronauts of Spaceship Earth, and we must carefully manage its limited resources.

To better understand this point, let's ask one very important question: what does well-being mean? Not simply individual well-being, but well-being of all the Earth's inhabitants? Is it just a matter of money or is there more to it? In other words, if everyone had the money to buy everything, could the current economic model based on the ownership of things satisfy all our needs?

Let's try to find the answer with a simple example. On Spaceship Earth today, there are about 1.1 billion cars and approximately 300 million buses, vans, and trucks (plus 600 million motorcycles). These 1.4 billion vehicles travel on about 64 million kilometers of roads. So, if all these vehicles were on the road, this would mean over 22 vehicles per kilometer. This might not seem like a lot but it is, when you consider that traffic congestion starts at about 50 vehicles per kilometer (25 per lane, considering the average number of lanes is 2). Suppose that by 2050 another 6 million kilometers of roads will have been built (an exaggerated estimate, by the way), reaching a total of 70 million kilometers. Multiplying this distance by 50, the number of vehicles that can be put on the road is far less than 2.8 billion. So, when the planet hosts 10 billion people, how can everyone own a car? How will we decide who can own a car, assuming everyone could afford one? This rough calculation suggests that a commodity like a car cannot be owned in the future, but will have to be used like a bus, a train, or a plane. From this simple example, we can see that attempting to significantly increase the distribution of wealth *without changing the economic model* could have catastrophic social and environmental consequences.

So, how can we change this model in order to achieve a better distribution of wealth, but without destructive effects? Clearly, we have to move from a production model that values the product to a new production model that values the *result* obtained from the product. We humans need to realize that intangible needs are more important than tangible needs; simply put, we need to travel, not to own a car; we need warm water, not to own a boiler, etc... The positive aspect is that the new generations, millennials and especially Generation Z, are moving in this direction, having been born into an already digital world. Moreover, the transition from satisfying basic needs to satisfying tangible needs, and then intangible needs, is simply the result of our evolution.

The real value lies not in ownership but in use. With the advent of the industrial production model all the value has been concentrated on ownership, even though it is well known in economics that service models are more profitable than models based on product sales. Why then didn't we focus on use from the start? The reason is simple: digital technologies have only reached full maturity in the last decade, so even at the start of this century the shift from selling the product to selling the use of the product (the servitization of products) was unimaginable.

Until now, the absence of technologies for managing the product as a service has forced companies to 'dispose' of the product through its sale, thus transferring ownership to the consumer (incidentally, this transfer relieves the producer of all burdens and places them on the consumer). The paradox is that industrial machinery is purchased to maximize its use in the long term, while the products manufactured with these machines are made neither for the maximization of their use nor to last forever, but to be consumed quickly and replaced as soon as possible, or to be displayed as status symbols.

The economy of the tangible has made us forget that the reason we buy products is not necessarily or exclusively to relish their ownership, but because they perform a useful function. We don't buy a car with the intention of keeping it parked (if we do the math, we'll find that a car's usage time is about an hour a day), but to travel with some comfort from one place to another.

A new economy based on a digital production model is possible if well-being is measured by access to goods rather than by ownership of goods. A result-based or performance-based economy is sustainable because it benefits companies (shareholders and employees), the people (who become customers instead of consumers), and the environment, as much more can be done with much less matter.

In the industrial production model, in order to reduce resource use and create more wealth, we are forced to increase the selling price of products, which is the exact opposite of what we need to do: to increase consumption, we have to lower the purchase price. But lowering the purchase price means reducing production costs, i.e., relocating to countries with low labor cost, using a greater amount of raw materials and finding ways to reduce their cost, again with many negative consequences for the people and the planet.

Today a paradigm shift is finally made possible by the new digital technologies, because we can increase the selling price per kilo without impacting consumers. This can be achieved simply by transforming consumers into users, that is, by selling them the use of products instead of the products themselves. In the usership economy, companies can earn more and distribute more wealth to their collaborators, while also preserving the planet, because they need less matter and less energy and produce less waste. On the customer side, more people can access goods at reasonable prices: no need to spend large amounts of money to become owners, and no need to bear all the burdens associated with ownership. Moreover, this virtuous circle transforms the economy from linear to circular, for its own convenience and benefit.

Increasing the selling price per kilo is fundamental for the sustainability of the planet, and the servitization of goods is the recipe for not transferring this price increase onto the consumer, who becomes a user instead. As a user, he can now enjoy the performance provided by the product at a much lower cost, while companies make higher profits, and the environment is preserved. A radical change of production model is advantageous for Profits, for People and for the Planet, and this is what digital technologies are encouraging us to do.

PART I

It's all about sustainability

*You never change things by fighting the existing reality.
To change something, build a new model that makes
the existing model obsolete.*

Richard Buckminster Fuller

1.1 The bill of the future, year 3000

I wonder what the author of the article "A.D. 3000", published in Harper's Magazine[1] in January 1856, would say if he could see today's world. The writer imagined waking up in the year 3000 and described everyday life in the future.

Among other things, he envisioned entering a café, ordering a glass of water and being astounded by the sight of the bill. For a simple glass of water, the items listed on the $7.27 bill referred to various services such as the waiter's repeated bows upon entrance, the attendant opening the door, the use of the table and chair, while the only product effectively sold, the spring water poured into the glass and consumed, amounted to a mere $0.02.

This was a very far-sighted vision of the world of the intangible, a world this book attempts to analyze. As far back as 1856, well before the advent of computers and of the Internet, some people were able to imagine an economy where the intangible would prevail over the tangible. A truly anticipatory vision for those years.

We are not yet in the year 3000, and while the industry persists in its mistrust of services, often seen as antagonists of products, the author of the above article would be astonished by the fact that within the present decade the fusion of products and services will become a reality. A reality made possible by the technological advances and transformations that are taking place, and first and foremost by digital technology.

---

[1] "A.D. 3000" in Harper's New Monthly Magazine, vol. XII, no. LXVIII, Jan. 1856

Digital technology changes the relationship between product and service, slowly uniting them in an indissoluble bond: this process, called **servitization**, is the focus of this book. We are on the brink of a great democratic transformation that customers will witness in terms of user experience and access to the use of products, while companies will have to rethink business models, value, products and production processes from the bottom up.

With the help of digital technologies, the utilization of products (servitization) will slowly prevail over outright ownership of products, thus marking the final transition from the era of industrial production to the era of digital production.

For the sake of clarity, when I speak of digital production I am referring to how digital technologies, which were meant initially to intensify production processes, have modified over time the very essence of the production modes, which now use information technology, cybernetics and knowledge both as factors of production and as means of production[2].

This is what I mean by 'digital mode of production': an impending and unavoidable change feared by some, rejected by others, yet upheld by our compelling need to make our industrial development model sustainable.

Implementing this change will also require a change in mindset, a new way of living and thinking which can already be seen in younger generations. Millennials (Gen Y) for instance are much less tied to ownership than previous generations, and Gen Z even less so. This evolution makes sense. In a long-forgotten past, with primitive technologies and low incomes, people's vision and interests were purely

---

[2] Masiero R. et al., *La società circolare. Fordismo, capitalismo molecolare, sharing economy*, DeriveApprodi, Roma 2016

local: the ownership of goods was the single source of security and was therefore considered a priority.

With prosperity, with the exponential development of technology and the transition to an increasingly global dimension of life, ownership tends to become a burden. Nowadays many goods are taken for granted, and there is a burgeoning appreciation for the opportunity to access them without necessarily owning them. Without this change in mentality, it would be difficult for servitization to take hold.

Products and services have always been connected, but the ratio between the two has been gradually reversing: the value of the tangible component of products is diminishing while the value of the intangible component grows.

The service economy already exists to some extent: many professionals sell services instead of products (doctors, financial advisors, lawyers etc.), and the transportation sector sells performances: when we buy a train ticket, we are not buying the train or even the temporary right to use it, but simply a transfer from one place to another.

However, in most cases people are still compelled to buy products when all they need is their use: they have to buy a boiler, a lawn mower or a drill when all they really want is warm water, a manicured lawn or some holes in a wall.

This is where digital technologies change everything: they are nearly miraculous facilitators paving the way to a new economy, where every product can be turned into a service focused on the satisfaction of intangible needs. We have already crossed the threshold of this new era. We are ready to move from the information society, where the tangible side of products is still predominant, to a super smart society where the intangible aspects become central. Through this fundamental shift, we can bestow on future generations a model of sustainable development that will generate wealth and well-being for all.

For any transition to take place four essential conditions must be met, and this also applies to the transition from product to service. These conditions, adapted from Simon Wardley's methodology[3], are listed below and will all be discussed in this book:

- **the concept behind the shift from product to service;**
- **the availability of technologies to achieve this goal;**
- **a defined, cost-effective economic model for the transition;**
- **a general willingness to adopt the new model.**

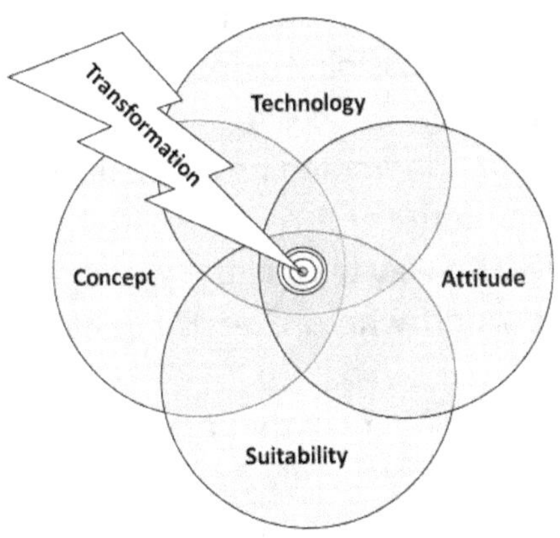

Figure 1.1 The four conditions for a transition

The fourth condition is based on a degree of dissatisfaction with the existing model. As we said above, young people are more oriented than previous generations toward pay-per-use

---

[3] Wardley S., Wardley maps, Topographical intelligence in business, https://medium.com/wardleymaps/anticipation-89692e9b0ced

and pay-as-you-go models; moreover, they are far more aware of our present sustainability issues. The so-called "green generation" is changing its shopping priorities: 75% of customers aged 34 and under are willing to pay more for products that have a positive social and environmental impact[4].

However, it takes some time for all four conditions to be met simultaneously. As is always the case, the seeds of a technological, scientific or economic revolution need time to mature.

Let's look for instance at the progress of modern science. In the seventeenth century, Galileo Galilei applies for the first time the scientific method that we still use today. A few decades later, Newton discovers the law of gravity which opens the door to scientific determinism and grants mankind the notion that it is possible to apprehend all aspects of the world. Newton also introduces the concept of equilibrium, on which we base our understanding of the universe. In the early years of the twentieth century, Einstein's theory of relativity further modifies the way we see the world, although it is still a deterministic world where everything happens below the speed of light.

In the same period, a new theory emerges to explain how matter works in the infinitely small dimension. Quantum mechanics is revolutionary in that it violates the basic principles of a physical theory as intended by Einstein, which are the principles of reality and locality. Despite being based on Heisenberg's uncertainty principle, quantum mechanics is

---

[4] Nielsen, The Sustainability Imperative, New Insights on Consumer Expectations, Oct. 2015; https://www.nielsen.com/wp-content/uploads/sites/3/2019/04/Global20Sustainability20Report_October202015.pdf

the theory that best explains the behavior of matter on a very small scale.

The relativity theory and the quantum theory have triggered huge paradigm shifts in the scientific field; however, tangible applications of these theories are still relatively rare in the technological and productive world, apart from a few important cases. One of these is the GPS system, which consists of a satellite network sending time signals nonstop to GPS receivers on the ground, which then use the signals to determine a geographical position with high accuracy. Receivers today are so small and inexpensive that you can find them in every cell phone. Likewise, lasers and especially transistors, which are ever-present in all electronic devices, represent two of the most well-known applications of quantum theory.

However, the practical application of quantum mechanics is still in its infancy. We are now witnessing the birth of the first quantum computers, incredible devices which will contribute astronomically to the improvement of our lives in the coming decades: they will help us deepen our understanding of the world, especially on a very small scale, improve efficiency in many industries and enhance our quality of life.

Although they are infrequently applied, the relativity theory and the quantum theory have nonetheless contributed to the development of Information and Communication Technologies (ICT). The evolution of computers, of software and of digital communications is certainly responsible for a large part of the important and profound cultural changes taking place in society.

As we have seen, a vague idea of servitization was emerging as far back as 1856, but for it to become a reality, the four conditions listed above had to be met: the very concept of servitization had to be developed and clarified, the technological substratum had to be mature enough, the related activities and businesses had to become economically convenient, and customers had to be ready to favor utilization of products over ownership of products.

Today these conditions have finally been met: information and communication technologies are sufficiently advanced and their price has reached an acceptable level.

Whether the world of industrial production is willing to abandon Newton's certainty and to embrace Heisenberg's uncertainty remains to be seen. Quantum mechanics asks us to relinquish definitively our need for precise predictions and to accept that, unlike what we have learned from Newton and Einstein, the future can no longer be mechanistically predetermined.

Everything now becomes systemic and interdependent: the world is exposed in all its complexity.

The difference between the industrial production model and the digital production model is basically a matter of trading certainty for uncertainty. The industrial production model is static and deterministic, based on the change of ownership of the product. Once the sale is final, the manufacturer loses all interest in the product, because almost all the associated risks are transferred to the consumer. On the contrary, the digital production model is dynamic and involves a much higher level of indetermination.

As the manufacturer maintains ownership, the product is now an asset whose value is defined by the delivery of services or performances. In order to deliver these services or performances and to mitigate the risks associated with the use of the product (which is now a company asset), the manufacturer faces two fundamental challenges: the need to properly insure the asset, and the need to trace the asset and be informed about its status in real time.

Digital production is much more dematerialized than industrial production, and technological progress follows a trend that progressively shifts from the tangible to the intangible. One of the first, if not the first, to notice this trend in 1938 was the architect, designer and futurologist Richard Buckminster Fuller. The inventor of the geodesic dome and the Dymaxion House[5] proposed a new concept of living where the house is an industrial product, pre-assembled and transportable, and I believe he can also be considered the precursor of today's sustainability.

His vision of future prosperity took shape in the principle of *ephemeralization*[6], a term he created to signify the ability of technological advancement to do "more and more with less and less until eventually you can do everything with nothing".

Consider how intercontinental calls were made before the advent of satellites. A call from Europe to America relied on 170,000 tons of copper, contained in the transoceanic cables that connected the two continents. Today, a satellite that weighs roughly a quarter ton performs the same function with greater efficiency and much less energy consumption: a striking example of dematerialization made possible by technological development. This trend will lead to a much more efficient production of goods, which will preserve the planet's resources while at the same time increasing our living standards.

---

[5] https://www.bfi.org/about-fuller/big-ideas/dymaxion-world/dymaxion-house

[6] Buckminster Fuller R., *Nine Chains to the Moon*, J.B. Lippincott Co, Philadelphia 1938

1.2 Servitizing to continue growing

It was only in 1972, on the occasion of two important events, that serious discussion about the use of resources and the sustainability of industrial development began. In June, the United Nations Conference on Human Environment discussed the risk of resource depletion following the publication of a report entitled "The Limits to Growth"[7] (LtG), commissioned by the Club of Rome to a group of researchers at MIT (Massachusetts Institute of Technology).

The report, based on the World3 simulation program[8] - created by Dennis and Donella Meadows on behalf of Jay Forrester, professor at MIT and founder of system dynamics - revealed the following: in a Business As Usual (BAU) scenario based on the classic industrial production model, given the expected growth rates for the world's population, exploitation of resources and pollution would lead to a socio-economic collapse starting halfway through the 21st century, with the world's population dropping by half by 2100.

Notably, a shared definition of sustainable development was agreed upon only in 1987, when the World Commission on Environment and Development, in a document that came to be known as the Brundtland report, defined sustainable development as "development that meets the needs of the present without compromising the ability of future generations to meet their own needs"[9]. The Commission concluded that the world was not at that time on a path of sustainable development and that the current patterns of

---

[7] Meadows D.H. et al., *The Limits to Growth. A Report for the Club of Rome's Project on the Predicament of Mankind*, Potomac Associates, 1972

[8] https://insightmaker.com/insight/1954/The-World3-Model-Classic-World-Simulation

[9] https://sustainabledevelopment.un.org/content/documents/5987our-common-future.pdf

production and consumption could not ensure that the needs of present and future generations would be met.

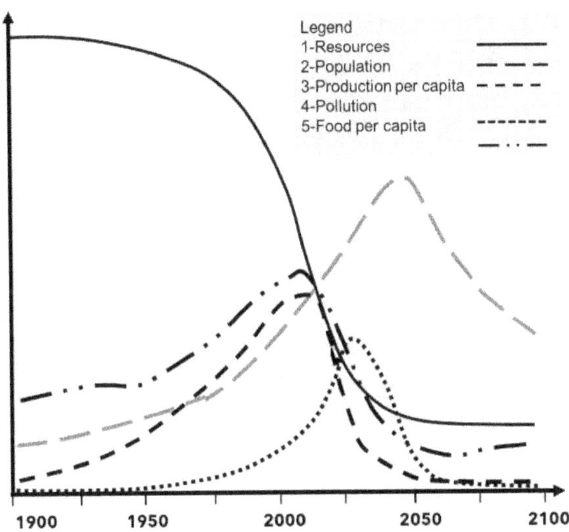

Figure 1.2 Visual results of the Meadows-Forrester World3 simulation (BAU scenario)

Many small steps have been taken, advancing a new awareness of man's great responsibility and of his power to change course and steer towards a more sustainable future. Aurelio Peccei, an enlightened entrepreneur who was a founder of the Club of Rome, expressed this concept eloquently in his autobiography: "My great hope is to have contributed - in the small measure accorded to a person - to the rebirth of man's spirit, without which the entire human system will revert to conceptions or extreme conditions which will lead it to ruination. But I have faith in man - and I believe in the human revolution which, even at the price of great sacrifice and suffering, will in the long run enable him to triumph"[10].

Fortunately, it seems that Gen Y and Gen Z have inherited Peccei's vision of a human revolution and are ready to build a sustainable society.

In 1988, one year after the Brundtland report, Sandra Vandermerwe and Juan Rada invented the term *servitization*. The first use of this term can be viewed as an indicator of a paradigm shift: products and services are no longer two separate and distinct categories, but they can be combined into one. Products as mere material objects are replaced by products integrated by one or more services, with services playing an increasingly primary role[11].

Services are becoming integral to any company's strategic mission; their growing importance signals the approach of a great transformation, a fundamental shift finally made possible by digital technologies. This transformation provides an extraordinary opportunity for egalitarian and sustainable growth for those wise enough to seize it.

The first step is developing products to which services can be added (also called service-oriented products), for instance, a smartphone with additional services provided through software applications (i.e.: web apps or mobile apps).

The second step is developing products that are use-oriented, for instance, an electric city car that can be rented for the time of use.

The third and final step is developing products that are result-oriented; in this case, customers pay for a specific result. For example, if we need a photocopier in our office, the seller keeps the ownership of the machine and is

---

[10] Peccei A., *The Human Quality*, Pergamon Press 1977

[11] Vandermerwe S., Rada J., *Servitization of Business: Adding Value by Adding Services*, in European Management Journal, vol. 6, no 4, Winter 1988

responsible for its maintenance, while we pay either a subscription fee or a monthly bill according to the number of copies made.

Note that there is a subtle difference between buying a product's use and buying a product's performance: in the first case, customers pay to have the product at their disposal, regardless of what they do or don't do with it; the provider's sole responsibility is to make sure that the product is in working order. In the second case, customers buy a specific result: the service provider has to guarantee the performance and is made accountable if the objective is not reached.

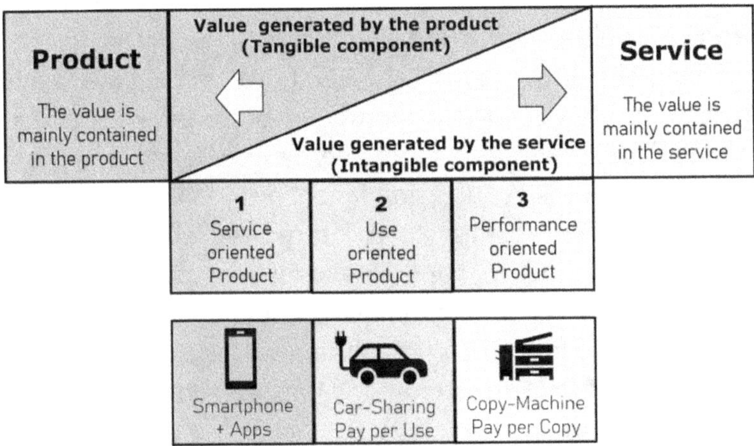

Figure 1.3 The transformation of products into services

Throughout history, humans have built social, political and economic systems in order to improve welfare and well-being. When physics began to reveal the laws governing nature, early economic thinkers looked for similar laws governing human society and the economy.

In this context, the industrial production model seemed full of promise, and it has in fact, despite its many flaws, amply contributed to poverty reduction. Nevertheless, in view of the projected population growth, we must now question its validity and recognize that it can no longer benefit humanity and that we must pilot a different course.

This inevitability was very clear to Orio Giarini, an Italian economist whose main interest was the study of social welfare issues and economic growth. Since the publication of the LtG report, many had begun to consider the end of economic growth as a looming threat, but Giarini held a different view. He understood that there were no limits to growth *tout court*, but only to a certain kind of growth, and that the limiting factors of the industrial production model could be overcome if we started to think of the economy in terms of well-being for individuals, for society and for the environment. In his book "The Limits to Certainty - Facing Risks in the New Service Economy", co-authored with Walter Stahel, Giarini writes about the limits to development anticipated by the World3 simulation in these terms:

"What in the seventies was interpreted essentially as a problem of limits to general economic growth, appears increasingly as the description of the end of the great cycle of the classical Industrial Revolution. This is what the simulations of Jay Forrester and Dennis Meadows point to. It is not the end of economic growth as such, but the end of *one sort* of economic growth, i.e., that based on the development of bigger and faster tools, of productive investments essentially in hardware rather than in software, in machines rather than in organization, in tangible products rather than in communication.

Obviously, an important part of economic activity will always depend upon tools and hardware, just as we still need agricultural produce. But today, hardware tools and agricultural produce already account for a *minor* part (even if still a relatively large one) of the work actually done in producing wealth and welfare. Within the most traditional industries themselves, as within agriculture, service type functions predominate"[12].

Giarini argues that contrary to what classical and neoclassical economists thought, we must not look for a balance between supply and demand: this balance can never be found because demand continuously selects supply. We need to move away from Newton's deterministic logic and learn to embrace and manage the uncertainty of a new world, the world of modern physics and of quantum mechanics. According to Giarini, "Newtonian man is powerful in his knowledge and his predictions but powerless in his actions. Heisenbergian man is powerless in his knowledge and in his predictions but powerful in his role as a participant in the evolutionary process of creation and destruction"[13].

The industrial production model is based on certainty, that is, on the sale of a tangible product with transfer of ownership. But this model is not sustainable in the long run, for two main reasons: first, because of population growth, and second, because a production model based on the purchase of products, especially non-durable ones, requires a huge consumption of non-renewable resources and inevitably results in environmental damage.

Walter Stahel, also an architect like Buckminster Fuller and one of the fathers of the circular economy, has thoroughly examined these topics. In "The Performance Economy"[14] he describes sustainability as the optimized growth of three dimensions: an economic dimension that must remain competitive, a labor dimension that takes into account social

---

[12] Giarini O., Stahel W.R., *The Limits to Certainty*, Kluwer Academic Pubs, 1989

[13] *Ibid.*, Giarini O., Stahel W.R., *The Limits to Certainty*

[14] Stahel W.R., *The Performance Economy*, Palgrave Macmillan, London 2006

wellbeing, and an ecological dimension focused on preserving the environment.

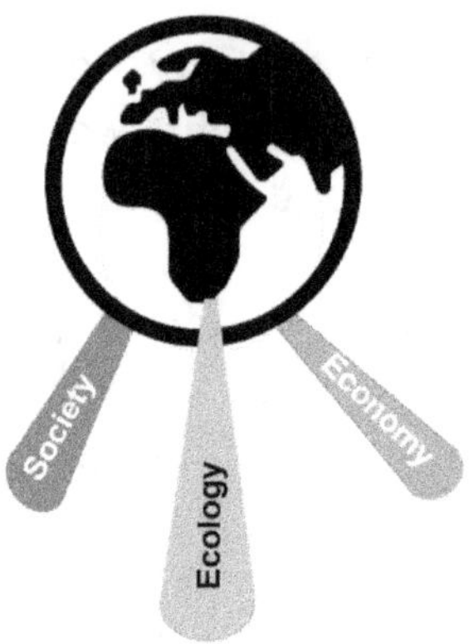

Figure 1.4 The three pillars of sustainability: sustainable action provides positive results for all actors (pillars)

In the industrial production model, the three dimensions are combined in an unbalanced and incompatible way; the economic dimension improves while the other two dimensions decline, and this decline is more than proportional, especially as regards the environment. In order to decouple the three dimensions in such a way that the growth of one is not detrimental to the others, we must implement a new production model enabling the transformation of products into services: it is an essential step if we want to ensure a continued yet sustainable growth, especially considering the planet's population increase in the last century.

The change of the production system and of the business models is enabled by three main vectors, described by Stahel in "The Performance Economy":

- **Using science and technology to decouple revenue and wealth growth from natural resources, through the** development of smart products, smart materials and smart solutions. For our purposes, designing and building new products that require less resources and are more reliable, long-lasting and connected in real time.

- Applying the business models of the service economy (of which servitization is an integral part) and extending manufacturers' responsibility to the full life cycle of their products, with a consequent increase in welfare.

- Increasing on-site job creation through the implementation of new business models which focus not on optimizing the flow of resources (as in the classic industrial production model), but rather on managing the assets produced (products are assets in the service economy).

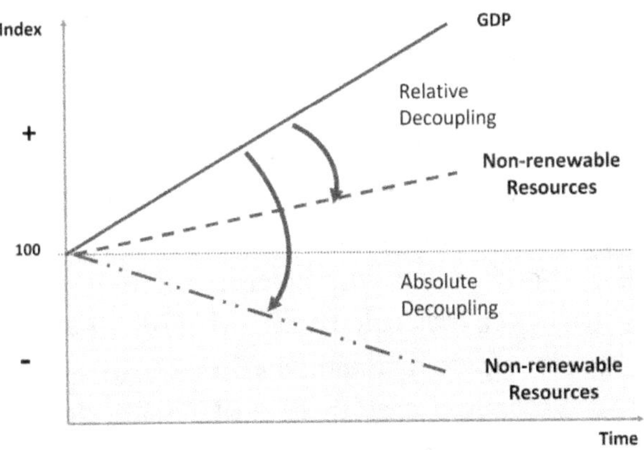

Figure 1.5 Relative and absolute decoupling of the production variables

The population growth trend is one of the main arguments against the industrial production model. According to data compiled and published every two years by the United Nations Department of Economic and Social Affairs, today the world's population is growing at a slower pace compared to the last century. In particular, the "World Population Prospects"[15] of 2019 highlight how the growth rate peaked between 1965 and 1970 with a maximum of 2.1% per year. Since then, the growth rate has halved, dropping to below 1.1% per year between 2015 and 2020, with an expected deceleration throughout the present century. Still, according to this survey, the world's population is expected to settle between 8.5 and 8.6 billion in 2030, between 9.4 and 10.1 billion in 2050, and between 9.4 and 12.7 billion in 2100.

When in 1938 Buckminster Fuller wrote "Nine Chains to the Moon", the title meant that all the humans living in his day, if put one on top of the other, would form a chain that covered nine times the distance between the Earth and the Moon. It took the whole history of mankind to reach 9 chains; today, only 84 years later, the planet's population would make 33 chains to the Moon.

To appreciate this impressive pace, think that we went from 1.65 billion at the beginning of the twentieth century to 6 billion in the year 2000, which means that we have grown 3.6 times in one hundred years. In the past twenty years alone, the total population has increased by another 2 billion and is now approaching 8 billion. A quick way to get a rough estimate of the doubling time given a specific percentage of growth is the so-called "rule of 70". This rule, best suited for small numbers, works by dividing 70 by the growth rate. For instance, if we have a growth rate of 2% the doubling time will be 35 years (70 divided by 2).

On average, based on the population numbers given above, we doubled twice in approximately 110 years, one doubling every 55 years. Inverting the 70 rule, that is, dividing

---

[15] United Nations Department of Economic and Social Affairs, Population Division (2019). World Population Prospects 2019: Highlights (ST/ESA/SER.A/423)

70 by 55, we obtain a growth rate of 1.27%. As we can see, with an average growth rate of only 1.27%, the world's population has multiplied by 4 in 110 years.

1.3 Sustainability and dematerialization

Although the population growth rate seems to be slowing down, it will not be possible to meet all its needs if the available resources continue to shrink. Let's review the global GDP trend. In 2018, the OECD (Organization for Economic Cooperation and Development) published a report[16] presenting the results of economic projections up to 2060 for 46 countries. This report shows a steady slowdown of global GDP, with a projected 2% decline as of 2060. The economic center of gravity will also continue to shift toward Asia, with India and China accounting for an increasing share of the world's GDP.

Our current economy is still based essentially on the satisfaction of tangible needs (on selling products). If we consider the consequences of population growth plus the effects on climate and on the environment brought about by human activities, we have to recognize that this model is no longer sustainable, in line with the LtG simulation in the Business As Usual (BAU) scenario. The LtG report presented many different scenarios, based on different assumptions, which were updated in a second book by the same authors, "Beyond the Limits"[17] published in 1992, and in a third book, "The Limits to Growth: the 30-Year Update"[18] published in

---

[16] Guillemette Y., Turner D., *The Long View: Scenarios for the World Economy to 2060*, Economic Policy Paper no. 22, OECD Publishing 2018

[17] Meadows D., Meadows D., Randers J., *Beyond the Limits* (Hardcover ed.), Chelsea Green Publishing, 1992 ISBN 0-930031-55-5

[18] Meadows D., Randers J., Meadows D., *Limits To Growth: The 30-Year Update* (Paperback ed.), Chelsea Green Publishing, June 2004 ISBN 193149858X

2004. In this last update the scenarios are based on a revised World3 simulation model that includes two new variables: the human ecological footprint and the human welfare.

Interestingly, the updated BAU scenario still leads to collapse like the first one. The same BAU scenario, but this time with twice the amount of natural resources available, still yields the same result, if not worse, proving that scarcity of natural resources is not the real problem.

Only two scenarios escape the economic collapse. One is supported by the rise of very powerful technologies in favor of pollution abatement, land yield enhancement, land protection and preservation of non-renewable resources; this scenario, while avoiding a downright collapse, still predicts economic decline.

The other one, called Stabilized World scenario, has the most positive outcome; like the previous one, it assumes that advanced technologies are applied to abate pollution, preserve resources, increase land yield and protect agricultural land, but it also applies limits to population growth and to the industrial output.

This is the only scenario which avoids total collapse and leads to a stable and sustainable future.

As of today, our course is not yet clear because the various scenarios evolve in similar ways up to 2020. It is only in this decade that we will begin to understand where we are headed. For the moment, we seem to be getting closer to the BAU scenario with twice the amount of resources available, but there is still time for a reorientation towards a sustainable scenario: a stabilization of the population seems viable given the slowing birth rate trends, and the control of the industrial output could be achieved by implementing the digital production model on a large scale.

Note that the industrial output per person can be reduced *without* necessarily limiting the satisfaction of human needs. An important thing to consider is that, fundamentally, most of our needs are intangible: we need *to write*, we don't need a pen; we need *to shave*, we don't need a razor; we need *to travel*, we don't need a plane, etc.

The solution is to find ways to satisfy these needs without uselessly wasting material resources, that is, by offering the outcome of products instead of the products themselves.

In the industrial production model, the goals of the two main actors are not aligned and can never be aligned: the industry wants to maximize short-term profits while humans want to maximize long-term well-being. Based on the way the traditional model is designed, two opposite forces are at play: industrial and economic priorities on one side, the quality of human life and the preservation of nature on the other.

Needless to say, the first side is much stronger than the second. As the goal of the dominant social agent becomes the goal of the system, there is considerable resistance to change and the sustainability problem becomes unsolvable[19].

As we have seen in the World3 standard scenario, in the classic model economic success implies that something else will have to be sacrificed, be it the environment or the well-being of people. This misalignment has always been present but, on a scarcely inhabited planet, it could be easily overlooked. Now, with a world population approaching 8 billion, the unsustainability of the industrial model stands out in a prominent manner, and this is where digital production can play an essential role.

When economic actors realize that they can make more profits by keeping the ownership of goods instead of selling

---

[19] Harich J., *Change Resistance as the Crux of the Environmental Sustainability Problem*, in System Dynamics Review, vol. 26, no.1 Jan.-Mar. 2010

them, this realization will automatically drive them towards the servitization model and consequently towards sustainability and the common good.

Thanks to digital production, for the first time in history change resistance can be overcome through a realignment of all interests. The conflicting needs of all actors can converge into a new system where everybody wins: the industry can continue to see profits growing, the environment is preserved and there is an overall improvement of human well-being.

However, overcoming change resistance also requires a "human revolution"[20], a shift in mentality and a commitment to adopt more virtuous behaviors. The human factor is essential, because in the end both consumers and manufacturers are human beings. Consumers must be willing to change their attitude and adopt sustainable habits, for example accepting to share a car instead of owning it, thereby becoming clients.

Likewise, entrepreneurs must meet these 'new consumers' (clients) halfway and agree to sell the use or performance of products instead of the products themselves.

Of course, this is not an easy transition for two main reasons: the risks involved in managing a service instead of a product, and the initial financial investment required to implement the new business model.

I hope I have clarified the primary advantage of the digital production model, which is to *simultaneously* allow the satisfaction of three fundamental needs: economic expansion, human well-being and preservation of the environment.

To simulate the effects of this transition in the long run, we need advanced models of future scenarios that go beyond

---

[20] *Ibid.*, Peccei A., *The Human Quality*

the well-known World3 simulations. Some new systemic dynamics models are emerging[21] but they require further refinement to fully incorporate the digital production model.

The World3 simulation has two significant merits: it shows that the industrial model leads to an unsustainable scenario, and it also tells us that there is light at the end of the tunnel, provided that we apply new technologies, limit the production output and slow down population growth.

Nevertheless, this model is beginning to be outdated and is not suitable for the simulation of a highly servitized society. As Giarini said, the collapse predicted by World3 is basically the collapse of one type of production system[22]. By changing the production model, the collapse predicted by the World3 simulation in the Business-As-Usual scenario can be avoided.

Digitization gives us hope that we can still build a future inclusive of growth by removing the limits imposed by the industrial model, but in order to do this, the economy of the intangible must quickly expand on a large scale.

This transition will lead to two results: first, products at the end of their life cycle will turn into resources; second, we will be able to do more and more with less and less matter, energy, time and space. I am convinced that it is now absolutely necessary to move from an economy of matter to an economy of data and knowledge like the one enabled by digital production.

To illustrate the benefits of an economy of data and knowledge, let's start by looking at the price per kilo of some products. It might seem odd, but the price per kilo of products is an excellent measure of the value of knowledge and/or of

---

[21] Pasqualino R., Demartini M., Bagheri F., *Digital Transformation and Sustainable Oriented Innovation: A System Transition Model for Socio-Economic Scenario Analysis*, in Sustainability, 2021, 13, 11564

[22] *Ibid.* Giarini O., Stahel W.R., *The Limits to Certainty*

the value of data from which knowledge is derived. To exemplify this, I have listed below (Table 1.1) the estimated prices of some products.

To grasp this concept further, it might be useful to look at any item trying to determine its cost per kilo. This exercise is essential to understand Stahel's assumption that sustainability involves an increase in the selling price per kilo of products, without a corresponding increase in price for customers[23].

This result is unexpected and seems paradoxical but can easily be explained if we consider the following: on one side, much fewer resources are needed to obtain the same product (thanks to technology); on the other side, the few resources used are further saved through sharing (thanks to servitization).

If we look at this through the eyes of industrial production, it might look like magic. In reality, this apparent miracle is the logical result of the two factors that are the subject of this book: digital technology and servitization.

Let's take for instance a passenger aircraft that costs about €1,000 per kilo and a smartphone that has an average price of about €2,700 per kilo. The airplane has a very high price per unit (for example, an Airbus A320 costs about 110 million euro) but it can be used as a service for a reasonable amount of money: an economy ticket can cost €10 to €150 per hour depending on the destination and the airline. On the other hand, a smartphone has a higher price per kilo than a plane, but it has a very low purchase price because, thanks to dematerialization (which is in turn made possible by technological progress) it weighs only about 100 grams.

---

[23] *Ibid.*, Stahel W.R., *The Performance Economy*

#	Product	Price/Kg
1	Cement	0.15 €/Kg
2	Inox steel	2.5 €/Kg
3	Cruise ship	7 €/Kg
4	Car (compact size)	17 €/Kg
5	City bicycle	20 €/Kg
6	Car (full-size sedan)	31 €/Kg
7	Home gas boiler	35 €/Kg
8	Locomotive	50 €/Kg
9	Razor blades	70 €/Kg
10	Analgesic/antipyretic pills	350 €/Kg
11	Mini PC	400 €/Kg
12	NotebooK PC	700 €/Kg
13	USB memory stick	800 €/Kg
14	Aircraft	1,000 €/Kg
15	Android smartphone	2,500 €/Kg
16	Haute couture dress	5,000 €/Kg
17	Branded solar glasses	3,000 €/Kg
18	300mm wafer, 5nm chips	120,000 €/Kg

Table 1.1 Price per kg of some products (approx. numbers)

As we can see, technology increases the value per kilo of products compared to the value per kilo of the raw material from which they are made.

Note that this does not happen for all products: some highly technological products, such as a modern locomotive or a car, still have a very low price per kilo (mainly due to the presence of metals that greatly impact weight).

The car example is particularly interesting: we will see how, thanks to servitization, its price per kilo can increase while at the same time saving customer money and reducing environmental impact. Some fashion products included in the list show how brand and creativity can also increase the price per kilo of products. Clearly, prices per kilo are defined not by matter but by technologies and creativity.

Digital technologies are extremely pervasive by nature, and they are leading the transformation of society currently under way. The Internet of Things, Big Data and Artificial Intelligence are all involved in this transformation. Thanks to these technological advances, we can now enter the service era, change our business models, and meet people's intangible needs.

The legendary Cray-1, designed and built in 1976 by Cray Research[24], can be considered one of the first real supercomputers in history. Specifically designed for scientific computing, it was an incredibly fast computer for the time, with a theoretical performance of 160 million instructions per second (MIPS). The Cray-1 supercomputer had: a main memory of 8 Megabytes, a weight of 5.5 tons (including the Freon refrigeration system), a power consumption of 115 Kilo-Watts, and a cost of $7.9 million without the disk memory (roughly equal to $30 million of today).

To fully appreciate the astonishing effect of technological innovation and dematerialization, just think that a 5.5-ton supercomputer from the seventies fits 5 times inside a high-end 150-gram cell phone made in 2010, with a compression factor of about 180,000 times in weight, 250,000 times in consumption, and 350,000 times in absolute cost. Today, any cell phone is hundreds of times more powerful than a Cray-1. Even so, there are no relevant changes in the price per kilo: the price of Cray-1 was about $1,400 per kilo, a little more than $5,400 of today, while a 2010 iPhone4 costs about $4,400 per kilo (luckily, it only weighs 137 grams). At present it would be hard to find a device with the performance of a

---

[24] https://en.wikipedia.org/wiki/Cray-1

Cray-1, save perhaps in a $100 thermostat, with a price reduction of 360,000 times.

If we compare the various functions of a modern smartphone (camera, recorder, GPS etc.) with their historical and inflation-adjusted prices, we realize that we have over one million dollars from the eighties in our pocket, not including the value of the computational function.

Product	Model	Introduction year	Historical price ($)	Present value ($)
Video player	Toshiba V 8500 T	1981	1,495	4,989
Encyclopaedia	Compton's CD	1989	1,400	3,425
Video camera	RCA CC010	1981	1,100	3,671
GPS	TI NAVSTAR	1982	119,000	374,095
Video conferencing	Compression Labs VC	1982	250,000	785,914
Digital voice recorder	SONY PCM-1	1978	4,400	20,472
5-megapixel camera	Canon RC-701	1986	2,458	6,803
Total				**~1,199,369**
Supercomputer	Cray-2	1985	~16,000,000	~45,109,739
Grand Total				**~46,309,108**

Table 1.2 Dematerialization and demonetization. Today's smartphone, over $46 million in the eighties[25]

In a smartphone, the computational power alone, which is the main driver of the app economy, is worth more than $45 million of the eighties, for a total value of over $46 million, not to mention the dramatic decrease in used matter, space and energy.

Buckminster Fuller considered research as an activity at the service of man's well-being. For this reason, he was convinced that research required a multidisciplinary and systemic approach. He had an intuition that progress in all

---

[25] https://www.discovermagazine.com/technology/our-wonderful-age-of-abundance-in-9-striking-infographics

fields always tends to dematerialize. As we have seen, this is certainly true for products; now we need to find a way to apply dematerialization to business models as well.

1.4 Technology-Biology: one to zero

Imagine you are holding a large sheet of paper in your hands. Fold it in half and then continue to fold it over and over for as many times as possible. Now imagine you could fold it fifty times. How thick do you think this sheet of paper would be? Probably, your instinctive estimate (not involving calculations) would be around twenty or thirty centimeters. As humans, we are used to perceive reality in a linear way and to misjudge the effects of exponential growth.

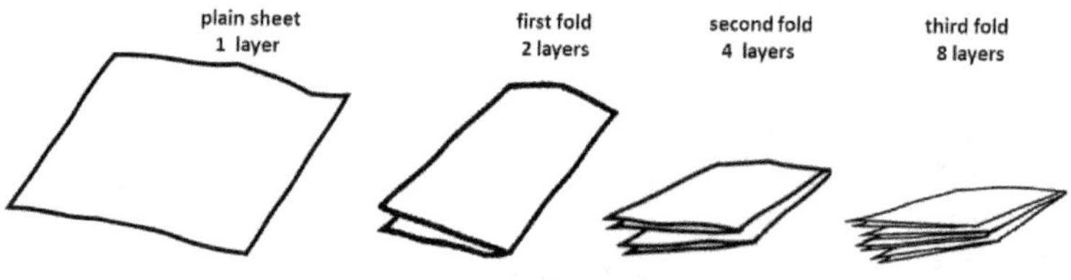

Figure 1.6 Each fold doubles the sheet's thickness

You will be understandably shocked to discover that the final thickness of the folded paper would be 112,899,906 km, close to the distance between the Earth and the Sun (149,600,000 km). This very surprising result can be easily explained: in mathematics, doubling the thickness at each paper fold can be expressed by $0.1mm \times 2^{50}$, that is, 2 multiplied by itself 50 times, and then multiplied by 0.1mm (or whatever the thickness is).

Technology works in exactly the same way. We live in an unprecedented era where rapid innovation gives us plenty of opportunities, but these opportunities are only marginally realized because we typically perceive the world in a linear way[26]. Even in nature, all phenomena have an initial exponential growth, but this growth later slows down because of saturation.

In the natural world, growth at some point begins to slow down, then it stops and decay begins. If for instance you plant water lilies in a pond, they will gradually cover the whole surface because they reproduce easily. However, their growth, which is by all means exponential, will be limited in time due to space saturation: once they have covered the entire surface of the pond, the water lilies will stop propagating.

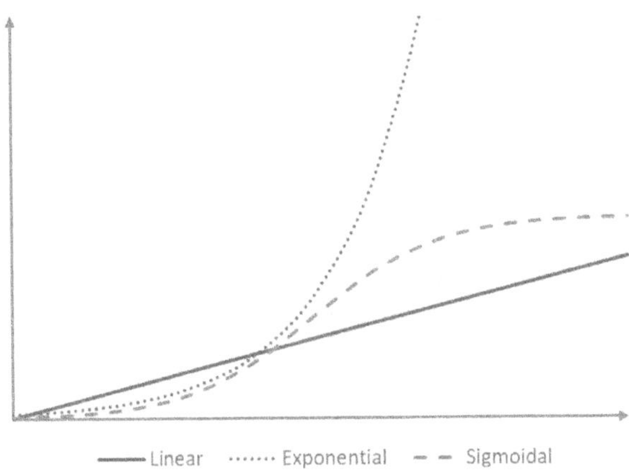

Figure 1.7 Trends for the linear, exponential and sigmoidal function

After a time, they will have exhausted all the available resources and they will begin to die. At first, the dying plants will be replaced by new plants and the situation will remain stable, but with time the water and nutrients will be depleted resulting in the death of all plants. This kind of growth follows

---

[26] De Toni A.F., Siagri R., Battistella C., *Corporate Foresight: Anticipating the Future*, Routledge, Oxon 2017

an 'S' or sigmoidal curve: the plants grow exponentially at first, then they reach saturation and remain temporarily stable, finally they decay and die when resources are depleted.

As we said, humans hold a linear view and tend to underestimate exponential growth, because in nature exponential effects are short-lived and always follow an 'S' curve of growth and decay. However, in the world of technology things work differently: technology is - and will be for a long time to come - immune to saturation, because innovation processes create increasingly efficient technological substrates that follow the *'less is more'* rule. In this scenario, the only limitations are dictated by the laws of physics.

Each new technology is able to do much more with the same amount of resources employed. In addition, when a new technology is born, it is as if it had learned from the previous ones.

Each technology pushes progress further forward, fueling the exponential nature of progress itself. In practice, the 'S' curves overlap each other, resulting in a growth curve that is overall still exponential.

This acceleration also implies a compression of the time intervals between one evolutionary stage and the next. In the words of Ray Kurzweil[27], renowned inventor and computer scientist, and according to his law of accelerating returns, "we won't experience 100 years of progress in the 21st century - it will be more like 20,000 years of progress (at today's rate)"[28].

---

[27] Kurzweil R., *The Singularity is Near*, Viking Press, New York 2005
[28] Kurzweil R., *The Law of Accelerating Returns*, 2001:
https://www.kurzweilai.net/the-law-of-accelerating-returns

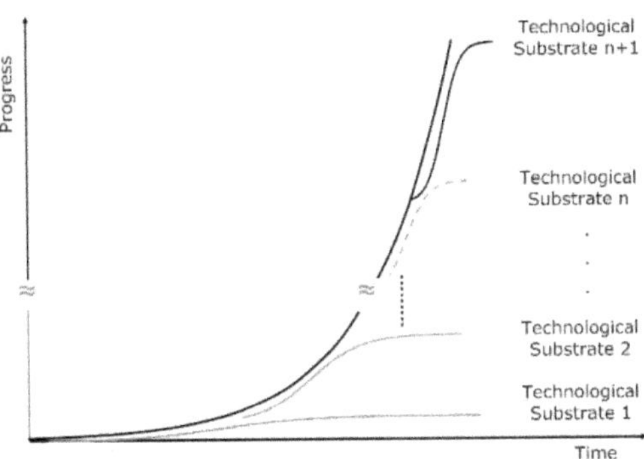

Figure 1.8 Exponential growth as a result of the accumulation of successive technological substrates, each of which has a sigmoidal behavior

Doubling its knowledge every 10 years, humanity will experience enormous growth. Note that half the total amount, that is 10,000 years of progress, will take place in the last ten years of this century. And beyond it all, the laws of physics will still give humanity further room for improvement and further means to continue growing.

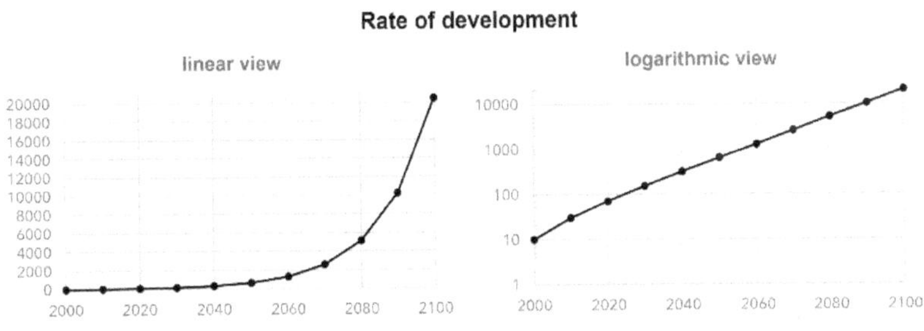

Figure 1.9 The rate of progress in the 21^ century: 20,000 years of progress compressed in 100 years

We are now at a point where innovation needs new technologies in order to leap forward and fuel new ones. We have digital technologies today that looked like science fiction just a few years ago. As the writer Arthur C. Clarke once said, "any sufficiently advanced technology is indistinguishable from magic"[29]. These technologies can help us change the socio-economic structure in which we live.

The process of technological innovation that fuels progress is independent of the will of individuals and is also independent of contexts. It cannot be stopped, because it is a collective phenomenon that affects all of humanity and in the long run will bring great benefits in terms of human well-being. These benefits are unquestionable: social change fostered by innovation can nourish new ways of thinking and new visions for the future, but it is not a risk-free enterprise.

The Florentine diplomat and philosopher Niccolò Machiavelli already knew this in 1513, when he wrote to Lorenzo de' Medici about the difficulty of managing change:

"And it ought to be remembered that there is nothing more difficult to take in hand, more perilous to conduct, or more uncertain in its success, than to take the lead in the introduction of a new order of things, because the innovator has for enemies all those who have done well under the old conditions, and lukewarm defenders in those who may do well under the new.

This coolness arises partly from fear of the opponents, who have the laws on their side, and partly from the incredulity of men, who do not readily believe in new things until they have had a long experience of them.

Thus, it happens that whenever those who are hostile have the opportunity to attack, they do it like partisans, whilst the others defend lukewarmly, in such wise that the prince is endangered along with them"[30].

---

[29] Clarke A.C., The three laws: https://en.wikipedia.org/wiki/Clarke's_three_laws
[30] Machiavelli N., *The Prince*, translated by W.K. Marriott, release date Mar. 1998 https://www.gutenberg.org/ebooks/1232

As pointed out by Machiavelli, there is always resistance to change and his contemporaries were not very different from us, at least from a genetic point of view. Still, a meaningful difference does exist, because thanks to technology, to digital communications and to the planetary network, we now operate not only based on genes but also based on memes.

Younger generations have a 'green meme': their awareness of climate change, biodiversity and sustainability will certainly favor their acceptance of the new modes of production and consumption enabled by digital technologies.

Figure 1.10 Average length of time companies remain in the S&P 500 index (calculated with a 7-year moving average)

The digital revolution is setting a faster pace for businesses; more than ever before, innovations appear in quick succession and the barriers to innovation are disappearing. In order to survive, companies will have to keep up with this pace, rapidly adapting their way of operating and their internal organization to the new production mode.

To get an idea of what is happening, look at how many years the largest US public companies stay in the S&P 500 basket, the index created by Standard & Poor in 1957 which tracks their stock performance. As you can see, the average timespan has decreased from about 60 years in the late fifties to about 20 years in 2020. This trend is solidly established and will be further accelerated by the effects of the digital revolution and by the paradigm shifts that come with it.

Innovation has a strong economic impact because each new level spreads the benefits and reaches more and more people. This is true with every innovation: the steam engine, electricity or the computer have all enabled an increasing number of people to do things that were previously either inconceivable, because they could not be done, or out of reach, because they were too expensive. Innovation not only allows to 'do more with less' but also lowers production costs for a given level of performance, like in the smartphone example.

The basic paradigm of innovation is to foster per capita GDP growth while at the same time producing increasingly affordable goods. This is evident in the figure below, which shows the steady increase of per capita GDP trend in the United Kingdom, where the industrial revolution began: an impressive achievement of the traditional production model of the past. Still, this does not mean that we must keep the same course in the future: affordable does not necessarily mean sustainable, and the sustainability factor must now be added to the equation.

The new course is not about chasing after the lowest price of products at all costs. It is about lowering the barrier to a certain number of services provided by products, with the help of technology. It is about a "good" price deflation. As we all know, the cell phone was initially available only to a select few; today anyone can buy one, even at ridiculously low prices.

Likewise, the day will surely come when we can go to the Moon at affordable prices, or even go and live on Mars in the city that Elon Musk is planning on the red planet. Whether we like it or not, this is our future.

Figure 1.11 Per capita GDP trend in the UK from 1250 to 2018 [31]

Peter Diamandis[32] describes the ongoing technological progress brought about by digitization with 'the six Ds':

- **Digitizing: everything that can be digitized will be digitized; thanks to the Internet of Things (IoT), virtually everything can be digitized.**

---

[31] Data source: Maddison Project Database, version 2020 by J. Bolt and J.L. van Zanden, Maddison style estimates of the evolution of the world economy. A new 2020 update.

[32] Diamandis P.H., Kotler S., *Abundance: The Future Is Better Than You Think*, Free Press, New York 2012

- **Deceptive: progress is exponential, but humans have a hard time seeing this, as in the example of the folded sheet of paper.**

- **Disruptive: when exponential effects kick in, the rules of the game change abruptly.**

- **Dematerializing: where they are applied, digital technologies always dematerialize in one way or another, just as Buckminster Fuller said.**

- **Demonetizing: dematerialization always results in demonetization, because the use of less material lowers the marginal cost of production and therefore the final price. This is what happens to computers according to Moore's law.**

- **Democratizing: all these cascading effects allow more and more people to access goods and services, and thus foster democratization. This is yet another indication that technological progress in the end will lead to a better distribution of wealth.**

I would like to add to this list a 7th D for 'Distributing': in order to achieve all of the above, the underlying architectures must necessarily become less centralized and more distributed. Although the evolution of computation is confirming the trend towards distribution as opposed to centralization, technologies have not followed a straight path from the center to the periphery.

It is more like the oscillation of a pendulum swinging back and forth: at every paradigm shift, the pendulum swings, either from the center to the periphery or vice versa, each time reinforcing one side. Over time, more and more computation tends to end up at the periphery, which becomes increasingly independent from the center. A sort of federation of computers is slowly being created, each with its own autonomy.

1.5 The disappearance of computers

Innovation and technology go hand in hand and take us to a new world which is less and less material and more and more digital, that is, increasingly made of data that can be transformed into information. Everything is shrinking and contracting, while the information content is expanding. The very history of computers is based on the contraction of four physical quantities - energy, matter, space, time - and on the expansion of a fifth quantity, information. Increasing amounts of information are coming from products, from processes, from human intelligence, and are also beginning to come from Artificial Intelligence.

Thanks to this increase, the compression of matter, energy, space and time has reached previously unthinkable levels: today's smartphones boast features comparable if not superior to the first supercomputers of the eighties.

How far can we take the miniaturization process? According to some calculations made by Eric Drexler - an engineer expert in nanotechnologies and researcher at the Institute for Molecular Manufacturing - from a theoretical point of view it could be possible to encapsulate in a 1 cm/side cube a computation capacity of one thousand billion billion operations per second[33].

To have an idea of what this means, suffice it to say that all the computers existing today on the planet, from the smallest to the largest, do not reach a computing power of this magnitude. In other words, a computer the size of a sugar

---

[33] Drexler K.E., *Nanosystems: Molecular Machinery, Manufacturing, and Computation*, Wiley Interscience, New York 1992

cube could contain, in terms of executable operations per second, all the computers currently on the planet.

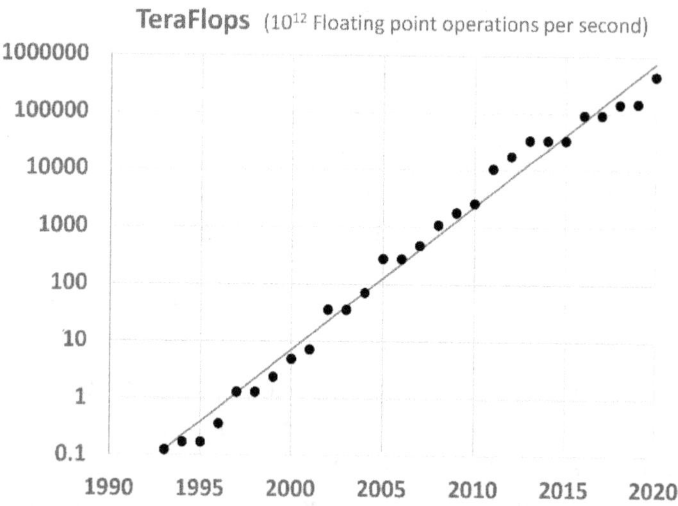

Figure 1.12 The exponential growth of supercomputers' computing power. Each dot represents the largest computer produced in the reference year. The line shows the increase of three orders of magnitude every 12 years

Speaking of power consumption, how much would such a small calculator consume compared to all the calculators in use today? The power requirement of all existing supercomputers, data servers, personal computers, notebooks, game consoles, cell phones, plus the communication network infrastructure, is about 150,000 Mega-Watts[34]. According to Drexler's calculations, a miniaturized computer with the same performance than our

---

[34] Interim Report for the Decadal Plan for Semiconductors, SIA, SRC https://www.semiconductors.org/wp-content/uploads/2020/10/Decadal-Plan_Interim-Report.pdf

hypothetical planetary computer would require only 0.1 Mega-Watt of power, around a million times less.

There is still room for improvement because, as Richard Feynman said, "there is plenty of room at the bottom"[35], and incredible opportunities are within our reach: sooner or later, anything that does not violate the laws of physics and is of interest to humanity becomes a reality. According to Seth Lloyd[36] - professor at MIT and at the Santa Fe Institute - with quantum physics we will be able to build computers with unimaginable processing capacity: by exploiting the quantum properties of electrons and of other particles which follow the laws of quantum mechanics, using only one kilogram of matter we could theoretically build a quantum supercomputer able to perform about 10^{51} operations per second.

In theory, we can compare the entire universe to a giant computer with a computational power of 10^{104} operations per second, which would have made, since its inception, about 10^{120} operations in total. Quantum computers are no longer very far away. Some are already operating, and not only in research laboratories.

These calculators are still limited in their functions and computational capacity, but the initial results are very encouraging. Before the end of this decade, I expect to see the first industrial applications, and shortly thereafter their commercial availability.

Future computers with extremely high performances will be progressively intertwined with our everyday life, so much

---

[35] Feynman R., Talk at the Annual Meeting of the American Physical Society, Dec. 1959 https://calteches.library.caltech.edu/47/2/1960Bottom.pdf

[36] Lloyd S., *Ultimate Physical Limits to Computation*, in Nature, vol. 406, no. 6788, Aug. 2000, pp. 1047-1054

so that they will disappear: we will no longer be aware of their presence, just as we are not aware of the air we breathe.

This explains the expression 'Internet of Things': tiny ubiquitous computers embedded in the things around us and constantly interconnected to the communication network. Their presence will improve our perceptive abilities and will give us an amplified perception of reality.

Moreover, not only will we perceive our immediate reality with increased intensity, we will also have direct access to more distant realities, as if we had suddenly acquired the quality of ubiquity. The new videoconferencing systems provide a foretaste of this: we do not have to be physically present to be present.

Thanks to the pervasiveness of computers interconnected on a small and large scale, reality will not only be visualized and virtualized: it will be augmented, and this will happen in real time. The satellite navigation system is a clear example of how these technologies are applied.

When we drive, our display shows the reality that surrounds us, but if we program our route, we can increase our perception. By using sensors that locate our position, our GPS tells us whether we will find heavy traffic or obstacles along the way and recommends alternative routes to reach our destination.

In doing so, the GPS uses lots of information that would not be available if we were using our five senses alone. Another technology essential to digital transformation is 5G: this new network is key to supporting and managing big data traffic while maintaining resilience and real-time.

This vision of pervasive computing requires many things: miniaturized computers on peripheral devices, high-performance centralized computers, communication infrastructures (the Internet backbone plus many other infrastructures such as 5G).

All are essential to support ubiquitous applications via Cloud Computing. This pervasive infrastructure, which I like to call 'computational exoskeleton'[37], will gradually extend to all human activities (some are already speaking of IoE, Internet of Everything) and will become the ideal starting point for the development of the new economy of the intangible. With the transformation of everything into a service and the spread of open-source software, a shift will take place in the economy: from being merely competitive, it will become both competitive *and* collaborative.

1.6 The laws of the digital world

The digital transformation we are witnessing today is based on three empirical laws that have been operating for several decades: Moore's law, Metcalfe's law and Gilder's law. In 2012 Professor Jack Wilson[38] described these laws as three fundamental trends: the growth of computing power, the growth of network value and the growth of total data bandwidth. Let's examine all three.

Moore's law dates back to 1965 and was formulated by Gordon Moore, chemist and co-founder of Intel. This law estimates the number of transistors on a computer chip, and states that their number doubles roughly every two years.

The accuracy of Moore's law can be easily verified with an example. Let's compare the processor of the 2010 Apple iPad and the processor of the 2020 iPad Air. The first iPad used the

---

[37] Siagri R., Pervasive Computers and the Grid: the Birth of a Computational Exoskeleton for Augmented Reality, ACM Proceedings of ESEC-FSE'07: https://dl.acm.org/doi/abs/10.1145/1287624.1287626

[38] Wilson J.M., https://www.jackmwilson.net/Entrepreneurship/Cases/Moores-Meltcalfes-Gilders-Law.pdf

A4 processor which contained 149 million transistors in 53mm^2. The iPad Air uses the A14 processor which contains 11,800,000,000 transistors in 88mm^2. Now let's do the math:

- **Number of transistors in the A4 processor: 149,000,000**
- **Silicon area of the A4 processor (mm^2): 53**
- **Years elapsed between the A4 and the A14: 11**
- **Number of times the transistors doubled according to Moore's law (11/2) : 5.5**
- **Transistor increase factor for same area ($2^{5.5}$): 45.3**
- **Correction factor for the area ratio of A14 and A4 (88/53): 1.65**
- **Transistors in millions, expected by applying Moore's law, after 11 years in 88mm^2:**

$$149{,}000{,}000 * 45.3 * 1.65 = 11{,}132{,}000{,}000$$

A truly amazing prediction that deviates by only 6%. We could look at any other computer chip, for instance the Intel Xeon processor installed on many servers, notebooks and personal computers, and we would find the same accurate correspondence between prediction and reality.

Needless to say, every time the number of components doubles, the computational power and the storage capacity also double, while the price remains the same. The practical consequence of this law is that, as time goes by, computers inevitably become smaller, faster and cheaper.

Moore's law explains the widespread dissemination of computers in every object of our life, from electronic toothbrushes to televisions, but it does not explain the soaring value of companies that were able to exploit from the start the Internet and the World Wide Web as a means of communication, compared to companies that only used the radio and TV.

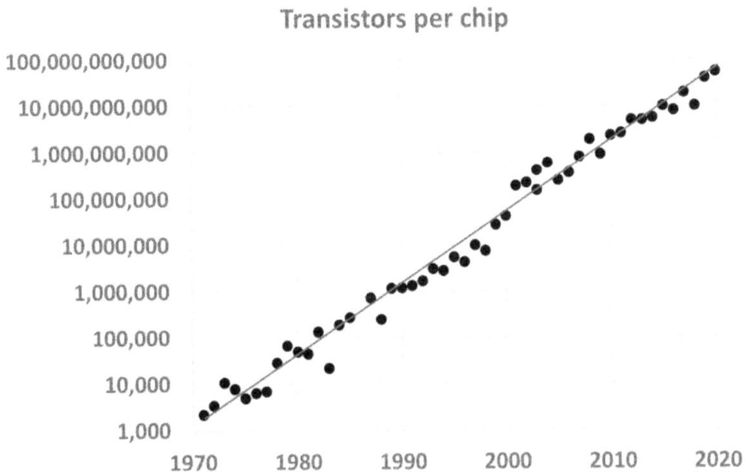

Figure 1.13 Moore's law, represented by the straight line. Each dot represents the number of transistors per processor produced.

To understand why this happened we need Metcalfe's law, from the early nineties. This law was formulated by George Gilder but is attributed to Robert Metcalfe, the inventor of Ethernet networks and an Internet pioneer. Unlike Moore's law, Metcalfe's law is not exponential but quadratic, and is used to measure the value of a computer network. It states that the value of a network scales as the square of the number of computers connected to it.

This happens because each computer added to a network uses the resources available in the network, but at the same time makes new resources available for the network itself. It follows that the value of a set of computers (node) connected in a network grows quadratically.

For instance, a thousand people on a network can generate about one million different conversations ($1,000^2 = 1,000,000$).

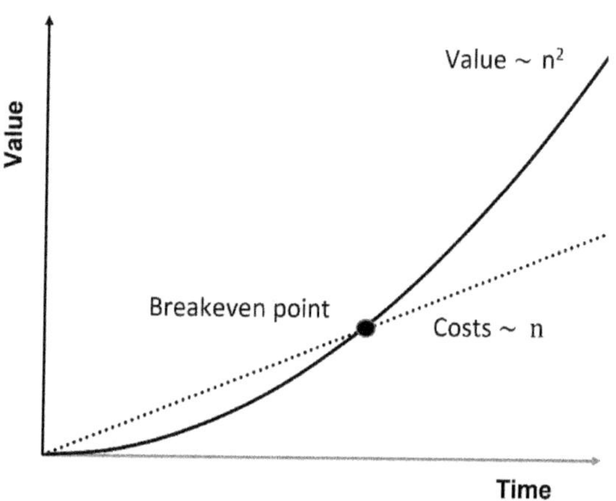

Figure 1.14 Metcalfe's law; the value of a network scales as the square of the nodes connected to it, while costs grow linearly

The combination of Moore's law with Metcalfe's law explains the Internet explosion and the great success of companies like Google or Yahoo in the early days of Internet.

But something is still missing: for a new digital and data-driven economy to develop, we also need an increase in data transport capacity, that is, a larger and larger bandwidth. The growth of total data bandwidth is measured by Gilder's law. This law was formulated by George Gilder, economist and co-founder of the Discovery Institute: it states that total bandwidth triples every twelve months, thereby implying a surprising notion, namely, that communication power grows at least three times faster than computing power.

This impressive pace translates into the possibility of transferring a huge amount of data at the speed of light. Without this exponential growth, Cloud Computing could never have been developed, because it would have been impossible to outsource data computation and data storage to data centers in remote locations.

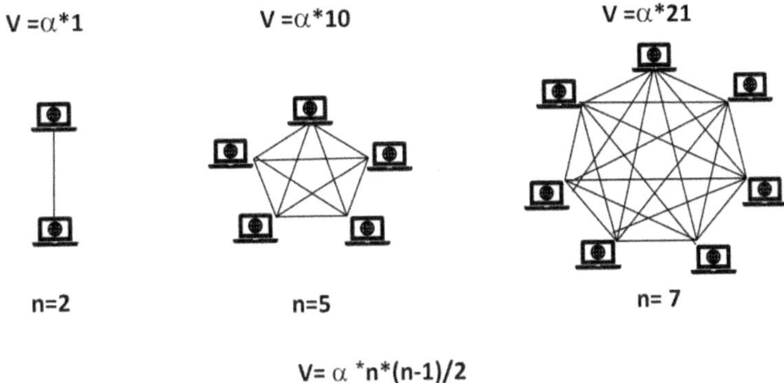

Figure 1.15 Graphic representation of Metcalfe's law

Let's return for a moment to the concept of network value. Metcalfe's law explains the initial development of Web 1.0, where it is possible to access content but not to directly interact with it. With Web 2.0 and Web 3.0, we have moved from a purely individual environment to a more collaborative one, where the boundary between data producers and data consumers is no longer well defined, and where these two roles become interchangeable.

Note that we use the word prosumer - invented in 1970 by futurologist Alvin Toffler[39] - to indicate a merger of the two. This new collaborative environment connects users not only with content, but also with other users. The most striking examples of this phenomenon are of course digital platforms like Airbnb, Amazon or Alibaba, and social networks like Facebook.

While Metcalfe's law helps us understand the evolution of the first Internet era and the attractiveness of the network, it

---

[39] Toffler A., *Future Shock,* Random House, New York 1970

does not account for what has happened in the last ten years; in fact, it apparently underestimates the potential value of the Internet as we know it today. To understand why, we need to take a brief look at the history of network laws, which analyze the number of possible connections as a function of technological progress.

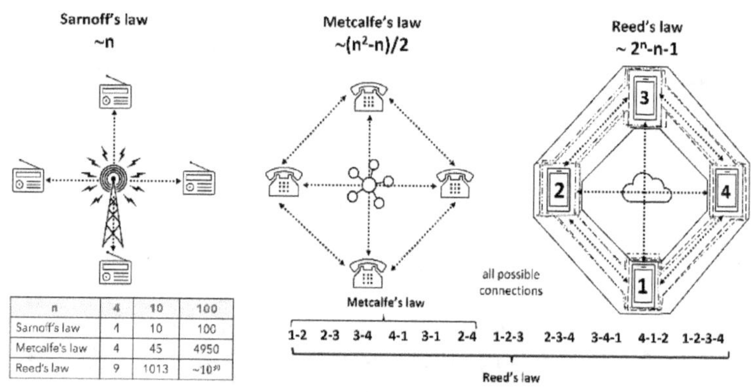

n	4	10	100
Sarnoff's law	4	10	100
Metcalfe's law	4	45	4950
Reed's law	9	1013	~10^{30}

Figure 1.16 The three network laws: Sarnoff's law linear, Metcalfe's law quadratic, Reed's law exponential

The first is Sarnoff's law, which dates back to the beginning of the twentieth century. Broadcasting pioneer David Sarnoff maintains that the value of a network grows proportionally to the size of the audience.

In Sarnoff's law the growth is linear because broadcasting is a one-way transmission, whereas in Metcalfe's law the growth is quadratic because everyone can potentially communicate with everyone else. With Web 2.0 and 3.0, and with the emergence of digital platforms, the interaction between participants in the network changes again and groups start to form, but this possibility is not considered by Metcalfe's law.

In order to address it we have to resort to Reed's law[40], also called 'group forming network theory'. According to this law, the value of large networks scales exponentially with the size of the network. Once the possibility of creating subsets of participants is introduced, the number of interconnections no longer grows linearly or quadratically, but exponentially. This explains the huge growth in value of digital platforms active on the Internet today.

In conclusion, to summarize: on the Internet, services directed at the public, such as news websites, increase their customers in a linear fashion; services based on transactions, such as email systems, benefit from a quadratic growth effect; finally, services that create communities, such as Facebook or Uber, can grow exponentially, according to the number of groups that can be formed.

What we observe, therefore, is that the value of a network of people and/or connected objects increases as it goes from linear (Sarnoff's law) to quadratic (Metcalfe's law) to exponential (Reed's law). If we want to make the most of this huge rise in value of online networks and translate it into economic results, it is absolutely essential that we advocate and encourage the digital transformation of companies and the implementation of new business models by every means possible.

1.7 A planetary network

The laws described in the above paragraph (Moore, Gilder, Metcalfe and Reed) account for the accelerating pace of technological progress. The most advanced business models are based on the existence and on the potentialities of networks, just as Cloud Computing. The cyberspace has

---

[40] Reed D.P., *The Law of the Pack*, in Harvard Business Review, March 2001

become an inescapable part of our reality and the economy has entered a more mature phase: it is now a true digital economy, where value is no longer found in atoms but in bits. A consequence of this evolution is clearly stated in the prophetic words of Nicholas Negroponte[41], founder of the Media Lab at MIT: back in 1995, he already understood that information technology would not only deal with computers but with our lives.

Bits, which can be defined as the smallest elements of information's DNA, are rapidly replacing atoms as the raw material of human interaction. Cyberspace has become a kind of planetary living organism: with uncountable networks of computer networks connecting a multitude of intelligent devices, it has the potential to amplify our abilities and perceptions, and to change our production models and the economy as a whole.

The intangible dimension that connects computers around the world and that we call the World Wide Web is the result of a recent innovation, but it was rather surprisingly envisioned a long time ago.

A detailed description of modern networks can be found as far back as 1955, long before computers and the Internet became a commodity, in the writings of the Jesuit philosopher Pierre Teilhard de Chardin[42], well known for his attempt to reconcile evolutionism and Christian faith. In his vision, a growing number of economic and psychic ties are forming at a faster and faster pace, so much so that with each passing day it becomes increasingly difficult for each of us to act or think other than collectively. This is tantamount to

---

[41] Negroponte N., *Being Digital,* A. Knopf, New York 1995
[42] Teilhard de Chardin P., *The Phenomenon of Man,* William Collins Sons & Co. Ltd., London 1959

saying that the advent of the Internet is unavoidable, a necessary step in the development of humanity.

This evolution, which could be defined as natural, fits perfectly into the lucid description made by the philosopher, who elaborates on the distinction between four consecutive phases: geological, biological, memetic and technological.

This last phase should lead to the emergence of the Noosphere, one of the most famous neologisms coined by Teilhard de Chardin: a sort of planetary thinking grid, an interconnected system of consciousness and information, a global network of self-awareness, instant feedback and global communication. It is not difficult to recognize, between the lines of this vision, the advent of the Internet, the broadband connection, the Cloud, the Internet of Things, Web 3.0 and Artificial Intelligence.

What has been said so far is well summarized by the five laws of technology formulated by John Smart[43]:

- **Technology learns about ten million times faster than we do.**

- **Humans are *selective catalysts*, not ultimate controllers of technological evolutionary development on Earth.**

- **Technology should self-actualize people and their cultures, not degrade, addict or enslave them, in 'structural violence'.**

- **The first generation of any technology is often de-humanizing, The second generation is generally ambivalent to humanity. The third generation, with luck, becomes net humanizing.**

- **Technologic innovation is progressively less disruptive to humanity as societies develop.**

---

[43] Smart J., https://www.accelerationwatch.com/laws.html#tech

When the first cars started circulating, a man directed their passage because they were seen as potentially dangerous. Later, cars became indifferent to humanity: we understood that danger existed, but that it could be kept under control with sufficient ease.

Finally (as we will see later on), the arrival of self-driving cars will completely change the structure of our society, proving the power of technology to create humanizing networks.

These introductory pages help define the conditions that have allowed humankind to reach this moment in history. Above all, I hope they convey a fundamental awareness regarding the importance of digital transformation.

Achieving sustainability, shifting from an industrial production to a digital production, transitioning from a product economy to a service economy are all crucial milestones that must be met if we really want to achieve a more democratic future and a general improvement of the living conditions and well-being of every individual on the planet.

We have explored the reasons why this transition is necessary and the trends that lead to servitization.

We have seen how computer technologies have evolved, permitting the development of large networks which are now driving the transformation.

We have also argued that the tendency to use things, as opposed to owning them, is quickly developing in younger generations, and this will facilitate the transition.

Finally, we have verified that the service economy is appropriate to the present situation, providing data to prove that dematerialization is the only sustainable option for our future.

Now that we have all the staple elements and we have identified the main harbingers of transformation, we will go deeper. In front of us, a sheet of paper scattered with dots: our task is to connect them and try to draw the shape of a new animal. At the moment we have only sketched its tail and paws.

We will now try to connect all the other dots and see the rest of the figure emerge. But do not forget that it will have to be a completely new animal, not the replica of a creature we already know.

PART II

The great disruption of the 4th Industrial Revolution

The changes are so profound that,
from the perspective of human history,
there has never been a time of
greater promise or potential peril.

Klaus Schwab

2.1 Children of an ever-changing society

We are children of an ever-changing society and always have been. The progress of society goes hand in hand with the evolution of production models. In the beginning, humans did not have a food production model that could satisfy their needs.

For hundreds of thousands of years, they did their best to survive by hunting, fishing and gathering. The first form of society, that we like to call society 1.0, was built around basic survival skills.

Quite recently, about ten thousand years ago, this subsistence economy slowly gave way to farming and to animal husbandry. It was a gradual but important transition because previously nomadic human groups began to settle permanently and to build the first villages.

This is the agricultural society, or society 2.0, based, for the first time in history, on a production model: a model devised to satisfy basic human needs. Until the eighteenth century, the vast majority of the world's population continued to make a living by cultivating and trading the products of the land, which assured livelihood, wealth and employment.

With the invention of the steam engine - we are in England in the second half of the eighteenth century - society changes again. Industrialization gives rise to society 3.0, based on the development of an industrial production model focused on the satisfaction of material needs and on the production of tangible goods.

The industrial period is complex and can be more easily understood by dividing it in four main stages, each of them initiated by a technological advancement:

- **First Industrial Revolution or Industry 1.0 (1784: the mechanical loom) - mechanical production (steam engine and water engine) replaces manual production.**

- **Second Industrial Revolution or Industry 2.0 (1870: the assembly line) - new sources of energy (oil and electricity) are introduced; electricity allows the development of assembly lines for mass production.**

- **Third Industrial Revolution or Industry 3.0 (1969: the first PLC) - Programmable Logic Controllers enter the assembly line to support process automation.**

- **Fourth Industrial Revolution - Artificial Intelligence, IoT, Big Data, Collaborative Robots (Cobots) all contribute to the development of cyber-physical systems.**

  - **First phase: Industry 4.0 (2011 to present) - Incremental phase following the logic of industrial production based on tangible goods (unsustainable BAU model).**

  - **Second phase: Industry 5.0 (from now on) - Disruptive phase following the logic of digital production based on intangible goods (sustainable model).**

Essentially, technology is the key through which we have accessed the era of the Fourth Industrial Revolution. This leap would not have been possible without the rapid spread of computers and of the Internet, the development of ICT technologies, and major improvements in software production enabled by Cloud Computing.

As of today, however, the industrial production model is still predominant and the new technologies have mainly been used incrementally, to improve operational efficiency (Industry 4.0).

Industry 4.0 is the gateway to a totally different and disruptive phase, which is just beginning to come to light: Industry 5.0[44]. In this new phase based on the post-industrial or digital production model, data, not machines, will be the primary elements. Once the digital transformation is complete, a new sustainable economy will be born, and with it a new society: Society 5.0.

Society 5.0 is also called the Super Smart Society; it is a concept elaborated in 2015[45] in Japan by a working group of the MEXT (Ministry of Culture, Education, Sports, Science and Technology), and it is also described in the document "Toward realization of the new economy and society"[46] published by Keidanren (Japan Business Federation) in 2016.

Society 5.0 is defined as a human-centered society that balances economic progress with social well-being through a system that strongly integrates the cyberspace and the physical space. At the heart of this system, and essential to it, is the digitization of all things.

The table below shows the stages of human evolution according to the Japanese and to the Western vision. We can see the process of human evolution as an upward spiraling movement: each 360° rotation corresponds to an era and the transition from one era to the next is increasingly rapid. Humans were hunters and gatherers for hundreds of thousands of years, then, ten thousand years ago, they became farmers.

About 250 years ago the industrial era began, and 50 years ago, with the Third Industrial Revolution, the information society was born. Everything is happening faster and faster;

---

[44] https://ec.europa.eu/info/research-and-innovation/research-area/industrial-research-and-innovation/industry-50_en

[45] https://www8.cao.go.jp/cstp/kihonkeikaku/5basicplan_en.pdf

[46] https://www.keidanren.or.jp/en/policy/2016/029_outline.pdf

the Fourth Industrial Revolution, which began only a few years ago, is opening the door to a great digital transformation.

We are now at the dawn of a new era, the super-intelligent society.

Evolution of Society	Japanese vision	Western vision	Evolution of needs
Hunting and Gathering	Society 1.0	Hunting and Gathering	Basic
Agriculture and Farming	Society 2.0	Agriculture and Farming	
First Industrial Revolution Steam engine and Mechanical parts	Society 3.0	Industry 1.0	Tangible
Second Industrial Revolution Electrical Motors, Electrical parts, Oil		Industry 2.0	
Third Industrial Revolution Phase 1 Electronics, Computers, Robots		Industry 3.0	
Third Industrial Revolution Phase 2 as Phase 1 + Internet	Society 4.0		
Fourth Industrial Revolution Phase 1 Digitization : IoT, Big Data, AI, Robots	Society 5.0	Industry 4.0	
Fourth Industrial Revolution Phase 2 Digital Production : as phase 1 + Cobots		Industry 5.0	Intangible

Table 2.1 Evolution of society and evolution of production systems

The western vision of the four industrial revolutions and the eastern vision of the five societies have been very well summarized by Pentti Malaska, a Finnish futurologist who focuses on the technological aspects of change as well as on its social implications.

His theory on the autopoietic transformation of societies[47] argues that human societies evolve in a gradual way and that each transformation has first an extensive phase, when it grows by expanding in the physical space, and then an

---

[47] Malaska P., *A Conceptual Framework for the Autopoietic Transformation of Societies*, FUTU-publication 5/99, 1999 -

www.utu.fi/fi/yksikot/ffrc/tutkimus/hankearkisto/Documents/futu_5_99.pdf

intensive phase, when new technologies are used to improve efficiency.

Hunters gatherers moved through vast territories in search of food. When the first human communities settled, agriculture was extensive at first, but as the population began to grow, the need arose to increase food production in a limited geographical area.

The shift to intensive agriculture required machinery and chemical fertilizers, which gave rise to the industrial age. At first, industrial production was also extensive.

Factories began to build and sell all kinds of products to satisfy tangible needs, but with time, in order to grow further, they had to find a way to maximize output on the same production area and to reduce costs.

The solution came from new technologies: process automation, computers and information technology opened the door to intensive industrial production.

Later on, the new computer and software industries, originally born to intensify tangible production, began to diversify their offer to satisfy intangible needs. This trend started with the media industry (videogames, software, movies etc.), and is now moving towards the transformation of products into services, which we could describe as extensive servitization.

Here again, the shift is made possible by the rise of new business models and by the advent of new technologies: the IoT, Big Data and AI. It is too early to predict what intensive servitization will look like. It will certainly be amazing and impossible even to imagine for us today.

It is important to note that in the case of the Fourth Industrial Revolution, the leap forward is not a mere intensification of the traditional industrial production mode: it is a totally new and disruptive phase.

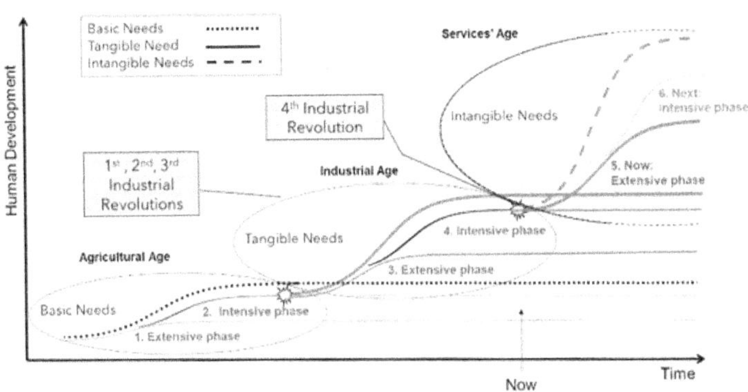

Figure 2.1 The stages leading up to the digital age of services, according to Malaska's model

A mere intensification would represent a danger for humankind because it would only exacerbate a BAU development model that is already unsustainable; it would generate advantages for the select few and disadvantages for the rest of us, worsen environmental problems and social inequalities, and cause the deterioration of quality of life, especially in the areas of the world where the cost of labor is low.

In Part I we have explored the complex problems of population growth, pollution increase and scarcity of resources. If we want to shift from the BAU scenario of the 'Limits to Growth' simulations to the sustainable Stabilized World scenario, it is imperative that we quickly implement new production and business models sustained by digital technologies.

We must accelerate the transition to the intangible era, and I am certain that the mindset of younger generations will serve as an important accelerator for change.

Also, we must not forget that all the LtG simulations are based on the industrial production model, not on the digital one. Going digital will align the interests of all actors (see par. 1.3), and this could be so disruptive that it might change the projections of the LtG reports and take us to the SW scenario more quickly than we think, thus proving Giarini's affirmation: "It is not the end of economic growth as such, but the end of *one sort* of economic growth"[48].

Let's now go back to the Fourth Industrial Revolution and see how it is expected to evolve over time. The World Economic Forum[49], in collaboration with Accenture, has outlined the four stages of its development. The first two are short-term stages and correspond to our definition of Industry 4.0, while the other two are medium-term stages and correspond to our definition of Industry 5.0 (see Fig. 2.2).

In the short term (Industry 4.0), digital technologies will first be used to increase production efficiency within the current industrial production model. Then, a progressive combination of products and services will take place, where products will be service-oriented.

The objects produced at this stage will be configured for connection, although not always connected. This phase remains mainly in a BAU scenario.

The really smart thing will happen soon thereafter (Industry 5.0), when digitized factories and products will be the norm. In this situation a new generation of entrepreneurs, eager to satisfy a new generation of clients, will begin to change the business model and to sell the product's outcome or the product's performance instead of the product itself. At this point, the transition to the so-called

---

[48] *Ibid.*, Giarini O., Stahel W.R., *The Limits to Certainty*

[49] WEF Report, Industrial Internet of Things: Unleashing the Potential of Connected Products and Services, 2015

https://www3.weforum.org/docs/WEFUSA_IndustrialInternet_Report2015.pdf

outcome economy (performance economy based on the definition of Walter Stahel) will be complete.

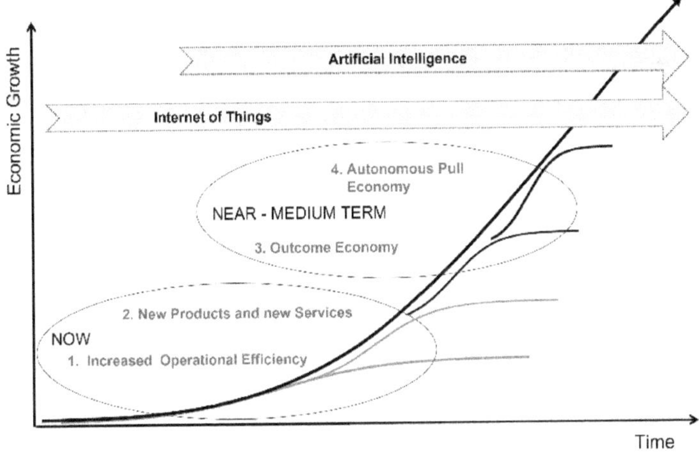

Figure 2.2 The four stages of the Fourth Industrial Revolution

The transition to the outcome economy will allow us to do everything we did before, only in a much better and sustainable manner. The outcome economy will open the door to the era of intangible assets. From there, it will be easy to implement a fully automated, demand-driven production mode that will be both highly sustainable and client-friendly. With a fully functioning digital production mode available, industrial production will seem like a distant past.

The problems with the present situation, where production is supply-driven, are there for all to see:

"Disconnected design, development, procurement, manufacturing, logistics, warehousing, and retailing processes mean overstocking or understocking are both common.

And bottlenecks and delays mean replenishment often comes too late, or obsolete products are left to clog shelves and stock rooms, before eventually finding their way to landfill sites"[50].

With widespread digitization, production will inevitably become demand-driven, and this for two reasons: first, because it will be much easier to have a reliable prediction on the actual demand, second, because customers will participate in the process of design and production (i.e. co-creation).

Digital production will steer the economy away from the mass standardization intrinsic to the first three industrial revolutions and towards the mass customization of the Fourth Industrial Revolution.

2.2 Digitization is a common resource

I would like to begin this paragraph with an important message: if we persist in projecting all the implications of new technologies, especially of Artificial Intelligence, into the traditional industrial model of goods production and sale, we will remain confined to a sterile model which will increasingly generate challenges and disadvantages for all, starting with environmental deterioration due to the excessive use of resources.

The rush to lower production costs will become unstoppable, man will increasingly be replaced by machines, and with no services linked to products it will be difficult to create new jobs and to save the planet from the depletion of its resources.

The greatest advantage of the service society is precisely that, since it offers countless services for the satisfaction of intangible needs, it also generates a vast number of new jobs

---

[50] https://www.theinterline.com/06/2020/from-push-to-pull-how-technology-promises-to-reverse-the-flow-of-production/

that only humans can perform[51]. In the service economy, jobs will be better paid and people will work less, because the human resource will become by far the most important one.

Service quality will strongly depend on the skills, knowledge and ability of employees, and the continuous development of these qualities will be essential to support the growth and expansion of businesses.

In terms of employment, it is easy to predict that offering highly efficient and functional services to entire nations will result in the recruitment of increasingly prepared and competent professionals to be employed in a variety of new jobs. If we take the United States and look at job distribution across the three economic sectors over time, we can see that the service sector is the one creating the most jobs. The more technology spreads, the more jobs are created in the service sector.

This phenomenon will grow as the economy becomes more servitized. In addition, as we will see at the end of Part III, servitization involves a rise in the selling price per kilo of products but does not entail a corresponding price increase for the customer who uses the service delivered by the product.

Thanks to the rise of the price per kilo, it will no longer be necessary to relocate production to areas of the world with low labor costs; on the contrary, companies will have to hire highly qualified personnel locally.

Wealth will be amply redistributed, not only because in a growing economy employment will soar, but also, and most importantly, because companies will see value in the welfare and well-being of their employees.

---

[51] Giarini O., Liedtke P.M., *The Employment Dilemma and the Future of Work,* Report to the Club of Rome, The Geneva Association 1996

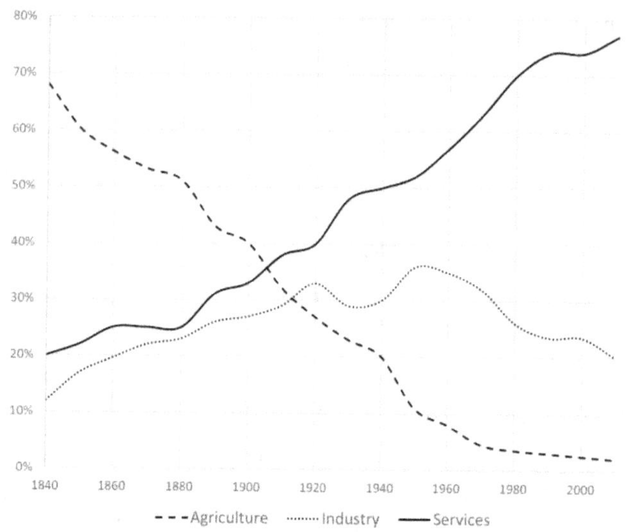

Figure 2.3 U.S.A employment trend by sectors, from 1840 to 2010[52]

Jobs and employment are a delicate topic, especially in these hard times made worse by the pandemic, but it is clearly a central theme for all modern countries. I think, however, that the meaning of work is changing, and that this word is now perceived more as a synonym of creativity.

Many activities and creative jobs that have a social or artistic value, like music or the figurative arts for example, are not fully monetized in the industrial society because they are not seen as providing economic value; in the service society, they will be much more valued because they will be perceived as essential to the well-being of individuals and of the human community as a whole.

---

[52] Data Sources: 1840-1900: R.E. Gallman and T.J. Weiss, *The Service Industries in the Nineteenth Century*, in Production and Productivity in the Service Industries, Victor Fuchs ed; 1900-1940: J.W. Kendrick, *Productivity Trends in the United States*, Princeton, Princeton University Press, 1961; 1950-2010: Bureau of Economic Analysis, National Income and Product.

Creativity is an important aspect of many people's life, and digitization will increasingly bring creativity to the fore. In this era of digital transformation, creativity is one of the few characteristics that are still essentially human.

This is why it is fundamental that schools modernize their teaching methods and develop creativity in their students, because this quality will be highly valued in the digital era. Unfortunately, there is a large discrepancy between the training given in schools and the demands of the economy.

Basically, schools were designed around the industrial production system and built in such a way as to provide suitable workers for the industry. Over time the industrial world changed, but the rigid structure of the school system did not follow.

Now, paradoxically, the productive world is rapidly marching forward while schools are stuck in a nineteenth century model, unable to keep up with the new economy, let alone anticipate its future needs.

Digital technologies not only warrant the satisfaction of basic needs; they also provide an answer to many other more sophisticated human needs. The economy of the intangible will necessarily have to take into account human happiness, which mainly depends on the development of individual talents, and human time will finally be given value, both in monetary terms and in terms of quality of life.

I agree with Roberto Masiero[53] when he says that in the industrial world, social conflict was about the relationship between capital and labor, while in the digital world the conflict is between true life and fictitious life. If we do not realize this fundamental opportunity, if we do not see the great leap forward that awaits us, then prejudice about the

---

[53] Masiero R., *Dopo la tecnica*, awaiting publication

dangers of digital technology and about humans losing their jobs to machines will continue to spread, and the public debate will become more and more fruitless and sterile.

We have analyzed the four industrial revolutions, we have understood what facilitated the transition from one to the other, but there is still one thing to consider, perhaps the most important, especially if we want to extricate ourselves from the many prejudices against technology that have consolidated over time.

The whole evolution of human societies has been at its core an evolution of social relationships. Each new step has encouraged the creation of stronger and stronger connections between individuals. In the hunter-gatherer society relationships were scarce. In the agricultural age humans were a little more connected, thanks to the creation of villages. With the First Industrial Revolution, cities were born and social relations began to expand, while remaining predominantly local. The subsequent periods have seen a steady increase in far-distance connections, and with the Internet the number of human relations and social networks has skyrocketed.

We are now entering a new phase (society 5.0) where digital technologies have the potential to distribute wealth more equitably, boost social cohesion, facilitate access to services, including transportation, and implement faster and faster planetary networks that will further amplify our ability to connect.

Human beings are made of relationships, as Italo Calvino wrote when describing the town of Ersilia: "In Ersilia, to establish the relationships that sustain the city's life, the inhabitants stretch strings from the corners of the houses, white or black or gray or black-and-white according to whether they mark a relationship of blood, of trade, authority, agency.

When the strings become so numerous that you can no longer pass among them, the inhabitants leave: the houses are dismantled; only the strings and their supports remain. From a mountainside, camping with their household goods, Ersilia's refugees look at the labyrinth of taut strings and poles that rise in the plain. That is the city of Ersilia still, and they are nothing."[54]

Digitization is a technology for relationships, the digital world is made of relationships, and humans have always selected technologies that increase and improve their networks of relationships, which reconnects us with Teilhard de Chardin's vision of the Noosphere.

Given the exponential progress of technologies, we might ask ourselves if humans as we know them today will actually be able to lead the forthcoming revolution. According to Giuseppe O. Longo, only *Homo technologicus*[55], a symbiotic being surrounded, supported, completed and even inhabited by technology[56], will be capable enough to do so. In other words, humans can only evolve by 'contaminating' themselves with technology and its innovations.

As selective catalysts of the very technologies that extend relationship networks, humans are the only beings that can dominate technology, and this will be done in the only way possible, through a process of symbiosis where AI will become indistinguishable from human intelligence. Humans need to envisage the possibility of being connected to computers and to realize that the human-machine symbiosis is unavoidable.

---

[54] Calvino I., *Invisible Cities*, Harcourt Brace & Company, New York 1974

[55] Longo G.O., *Homo technologicus*, Meltemi, Roma 2001

[56] Longo G.O., *Il simbionte. Prove di umanità futura*, Meltemi, Roma 2003

As astrophysicist Martin Rees once wrote: "Any creatures witnessing the Sun's demise won't be human— they'll be as different from us as we are from a bug. Posthuman evolution— here on Earth and far beyond— could be as prolonged as the Darwinian evolution that has led to us— and even more wonderful.

And evolution is now accelerating; it can happen via 'intelligent design' on a technological timescale, operating far faster than natural selection and driven by advances in genetics and in artificial intelligence (AI). The long-term future probably lies with electronic rather than organic 'life'."[57]

In this symbiotic framework, humans are invested with a great responsibility. If all these innovations are not used to promote the common good, reaffirm human dignity and safeguard the environment, there is a real danger of them being used to increase inequalities and restrict individual rights. This is why we should stay optimistic but also vigilant: as Klaus Schwab[58], founder of the World Economic Forum, declared back in 2016, digitization is a common resource and it must be treated as such.

2.3 Complexity and componentization

Something very specific happens in the transition between each industrial phase and the next. I am referring to combinatorial innovation, an interesting concept developed by Professor Hal Varian[59], Google's chief economist.

Each transition seems to be triggered by a phenomenon that we might call 'componentization': at a certain point,

---

[57] Rees M., *On the Future: Prospects for Humanity*, Princeton Univ. Press, 2018
[58] Schwab K., *The Fourth Industrial Revolution*, World Economic Forum 2016
[59] Varian H.R. et al. *The Economics of Information Technology*, Cambridge Univ. Press 2004

some components of a process become standard, and therefore can be easily combined and recombined to make new processes and new products. It is from this possibility that innovation arises.

Another way of looking at componentization has been provided by Herbert Simon[60], Nobel Prize laureate in Economic Sciences in 1978, and creator of a well-known theory of complex systems. In any field, from the self-driving car to the blockchain, simple systems tend with time to become complex; this is why we need a method to manage this growing complexity.

For Simon, the number one rule for managing a complex system is to break it down into highly autonomous subsystems that require only a loose interaction with each other to produce the required complexity. To explain this method, Simon resorts to the parable of the two watchmakers.

There once were two watchmakers, Hora and Tempus, who were both very good and made very fine watches. But while Hora prospered, Tempus became poorer and poorer, until he had to close shop. How so? The watches they both made consisted of about a thousand parts.

Tempus assembled them in such a way that, if while working he had to stop for a moment, all his work fell to pieces and had to be reassembled from scratch.

Hora instead had divided his work into sub-blocks, so that he was able to build the clocks step by step. If he had to stop, he would just pick up the last sub-block and go on from there.

The complexity was the same, but the job was organized in a different way.

---

[60] Simon H.A., *The Architecture of Complexity*, Proceedings of the American Philosophical Society, vol. 106, no. 6, Dec. 1962, pp. 467-482

The solution to mastering complexity is therefore to 'distribute' it, so to speak, into a set of subsystems, modules or macro-components.

However, this 'simplification' is possible only if the subsystems can be easily connected through a few well-defined points of contact, that is, if they are loosely coupled.

Everything can become modular, provided that the interactions between modules are all compliant with a predefined standard, just like Lego bricks: they are all different, but they all fit into the same interconnection matrix.

Each industrial revolution is based on a process of combinatorial innovation brought about by standardization.

The first transition from craftsmanship to industrial production was made possible by the standardization of mechanical parts. The shift from mechanical parts to mechanical systems produced new and more efficient machines: no longer forced to focus on single details, humans had more freedom to combine parts in different ways and create new and more complex objects.

The Second Industrial Revolution was based on the discovery of electricity: electrical parts such as motors were invented and slowly became standard. Machines were no longer purely mechanical; a vast array of electromechanical machines began to boost production.

The Third Industrial Revolution saw the birth of computers, which were built according to specific standards and could be easily inserted into machines and production processes.

We can see how the transformation deepened in time: the mechanical component began to decrease in favor of the electromechanical component, it was then further reduced in favor of the electronic component, all this with a simultaneous increase in standardization.

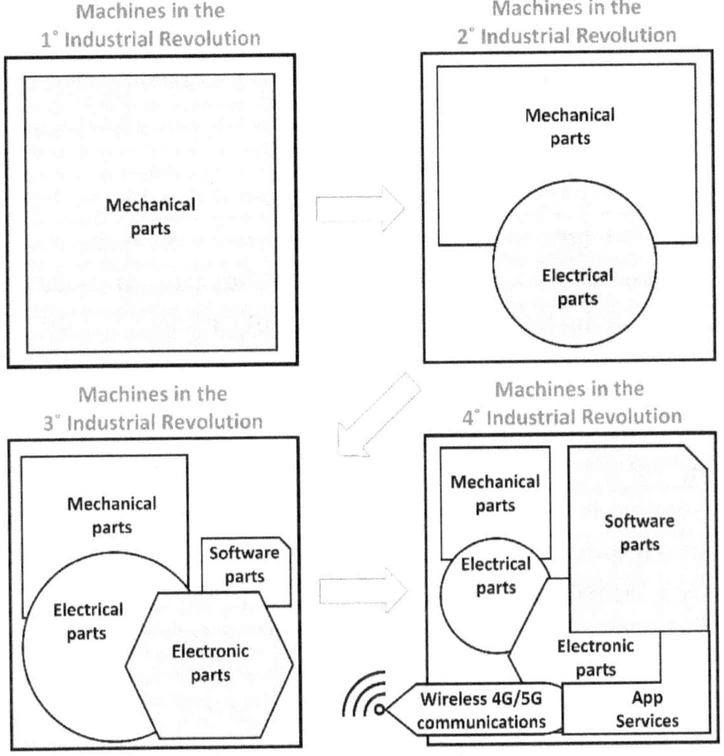

Figure 2.4 From hardware-defined to software-defined machines

Finally, the Fourth Industrial Revolution began, with a greater and more important innovation: the componentization of software. Software is now becoming modular and easily combinable, and this greatly facilitates the production of software applications that were unthinkable until recently due to high development costs.

Software is now much easier to produce and much more cost-effective, because components can easily be reused and aggregated in different ways to create new software.

Software is becoming the main component of machines. Mechanical parts have become less and less important while electromechanical parts have slightly increased, electronic parts have multiplied disproportionately and software is 'invading' the whole machine.

In 1970, electronic parts represented only 5% of a car's production cost. In 2020, this percentage had risen to 40% and it will rise to 50% by 2030. The presence of electronic components, software and communications is not just changing products, it is also deeply changing business models.

Look at Amazon, for example: is it a logistics company or rather a data and software company? and what about Netflix? Is it not also a data and software company? and Uber? another data and software company that sells the use of cars owned by third parties.

"Software is eating the world", famously asserted Marc Andreessen, US venture capitalist and Netscape founder in 2011, while interviewed for the Wall Street Journal[61]. The reality is that every business in the world is now fundamentally a software business.

In recent years, Jen-Hsun Huang - CEO of Nvidia - went even further, declaring: "Software is eating the world, but AI is going to eat software"[62]. And we will certainly need Artificial Intelligence more than ever to manage the huge amount of data collected from an exponentially growing number of connected objects (Internet of Things).

---

[61] www.wsj.com/articles/SB10001424053111903480904576512250915629460
[62] https://www.technologyreview.com/2017/05/12/151722/nvidia-ceo-software-is-eating-the-world-but-ai-is-going-to-eat-software/

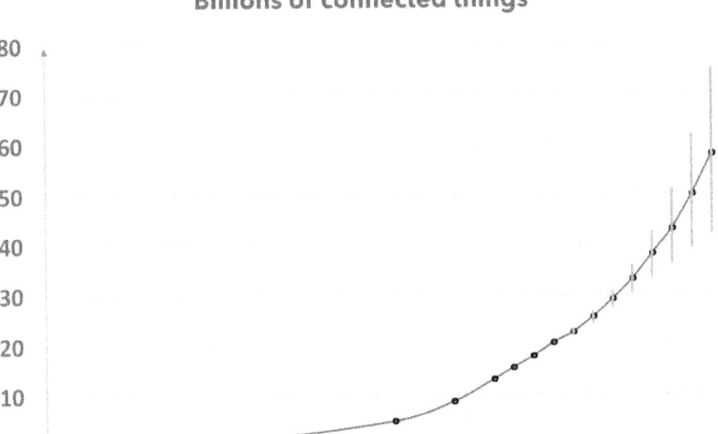

Figure 2.5 The exponential growth of connected devices

Some facts reveal the extent of this phenomenon:

- **We produce more information every two days than was created from the beginning of times to 2003;**

- **Every year, machine-generated data already amounts to 40% of all data generated on the Internet;**

- **Over 90% of all structured data in the world has been generated in the last two years;**

- **According to estimates, by 2025 there will be about 50 billions of IoT devices on the planet, generating about 80 Zettabytes of data;**

- **By 2025, the amount of data worldwide will reach 175 Zettabytes.**

Name	Symbol	Bytes	Power of 10	Analogy
Byte	B	1	10^0	1 character
Kilobyte	KB	1.000	10^3	~ 1 page of text characters
Megabyte	MB	1.000.000	10^6	900 pages of text
Gigabyte	GB	1.000.000.000	10^9	30 hours of Skype audio calls
Terabyte	TB	1.000.000.000.000	10^{12}	245 million DVDs
Petabyte	PB	1.000.000.000.000.000	10^{15}	Data produced every day on the planet: 1.1 Petabytes
Exabyte	EB	1.000.000.000.000.000.000	10^{18}	240,000 years of Skype video calls
Zettabyte	ZB	1,000.000.000.000.000.000.000	10^{21}	If a byte were a grain of rice, 1 Zettabyte of data would fill the entire Pacific Ocean (660,000 Km³)
Yottabyte	YB	1.000.000.000.000.000.000.000.000	10^{24}	22 times all the data on Earth in 2021 and about 6 times the data that will be present on Earth in 2025 (estimated: 175 Zettabytes).

Table 2.2 Units of measurement for data

2.4 From the cowboy economy to the spaceman economy

In February 2021, the European Parliament adopted the European Commission's Circular Economy Action Plan[63] to achieve a carbon-neutral, sustainable, toxic-free and fully circular economy by 2050.

Circular economy is described by Europe's highest institutional body as a model of production and consumption that involves sharing, lending, reusing, repairing, reconditioning and recycling existing materials and products as long as possible.

The principles of the circular economy are at odds with the linear industrial economic model, which relies on large quantities of readily available, low-cost raw materials and energy.

The difference between the two models has been nicely outlined by Masiero et al., according to whom the linear model means going, taking, achieving, consuming,

---

[63] https://www.europarl.europa.eu/doceo/document/TA-9-2021-0040_EN.html

eliminating, while the circular model means staying, adapting, using, consuming, recycling[64].

The economist Kenneth Boulding[65] first introduced the concept of a circular economy in a 1966 article in which he used a curious but effective metaphor. He described the two contrasting models as the cowboy economy and the spaceman economy:

- the cowboy economy is an open economy based on production, consumption and massive use of raw materials, which produces a lot of waste and pollution;

- the spaceman economy is a closed economy where production, consumption and the use of resources are kept to a minimum, and where there is a strong awareness of a limit to be respected.

In short, the cowboy economy brings us back to the traditional industrial model while the spaceman economy reveals a new perspective: a truly sustainable development model, where the circular economy will spread as a natural consequence of digitization.

The passage from the linear to the circular model can be represented with an analogy: the weight of the amount of data produced by digitization bends the linear chain, until the chain closes in on itself and becomes a circle (fig. 2.6).

The transition to a circular economy also makes it possible to overcome the main criticality of the classic industrial model, namely, that once the product is sold, full responsibility is handed over to the customer.

According to Stahel, the transfer of ownership from the manufacturer to the end consumer is precisely the aspect that has the greatest negative impact on sustainability. When

---

[64] *Ibid.*, Masiero R. et al., *La società circolare*

[65] Boulding K.E., *The Economics of the Coming Spaceship Earth*, in Environmental Quality Issues in a Growing Economy, 1966

ownership of products stays with the producer, new needs emerge: no longer using, throwing away and buying again, but using, reusing and recycling. The first consequence of this new approach is that resources cease to be wasted. As Stahel says, "the goods of today are the resources of tomorrow at yesterday's prices"[66].

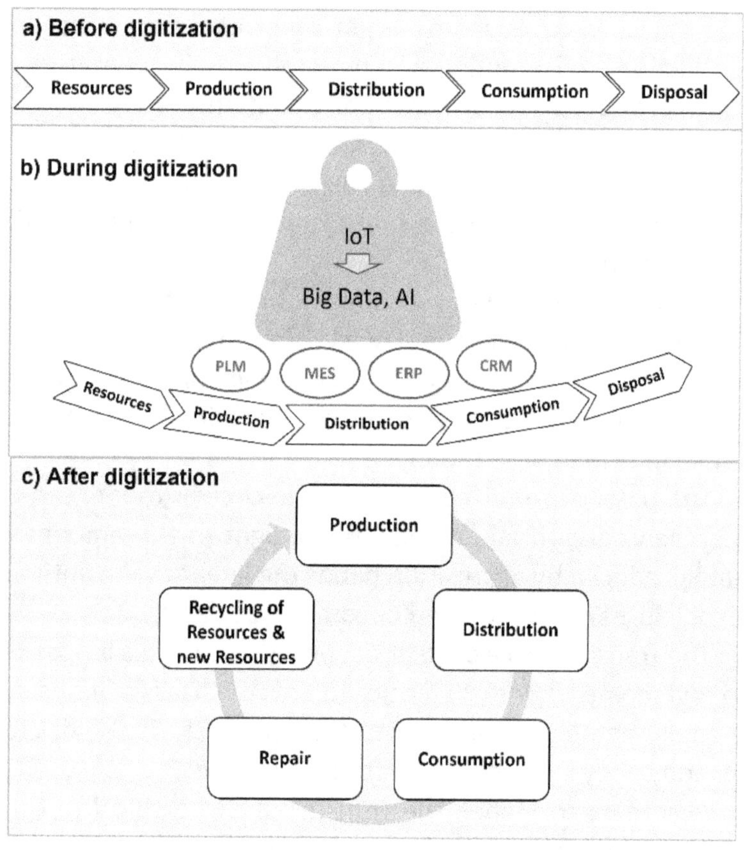

Figure 2.6 From linear to circular through digitization

---

[66] *Ibid.*, Stahel W.R., *The Performance Economy*

To achieve this result, we have to implement a new business model based on the sale of products as services.

By doing this, we automatically transition toward a circular economy, where the use of resources is decoupled both from industrial production and from social welfare.

Resources are no longer wasted because products are built using less matter, they last longer, they are shared among many users, and at the end of their life cycle they go back to the manufacturer who gets the material back without paying for it (as the product is still his property) and uses it to build a new product.

At the same time, all these aspects combined result in a higher price per kilo, which increases wealth and welfare because companies earn more, can pay higher wages and, as new jobs demand competence and creativity, must also find ways to promote staff loyalty.

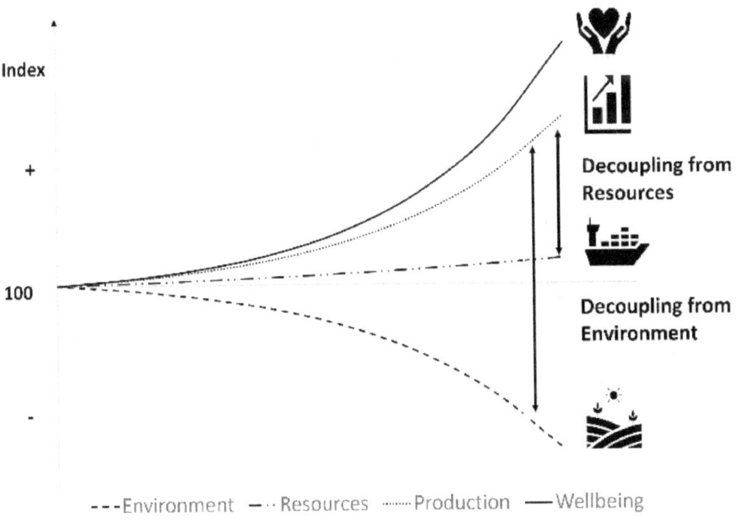

Figure 2.7 Decoupling production from resources results in diminished environmental impact and increased well-being

Applying this to a real situation, let's take the example of a car sold as a service and not as a product. Today a car dealer has one single obligation once the car is sold: to provide repairs or at the utmost to replace the car in the event that it breaks down under warranty.

If, on the other hand, the car is made available through a car sharing service to several people who do not buy it, but pay a subscription fee to be able to use it when needed, then the service seller will have to ensure that the car is always clean and in working order.

The very idea of designing and building a car for this use changes the production logic because the purpose is different. Nowadays, products have a programmed obsolescence, so that new ones can be sold in the medium term.

In the service economy, products will necessarily be of excellent quality: they will have to last a very long time, and in the case of cars, to consume little and pollute even less. These cars will be so well built that they will improve people's quality of life.

As of today, the industrial economy is still based on the intensive exploitation of resources, and consequently still impacts the environment very heavily.

In this regard, it can be interesting to compare the trend of the United States GDP with the amount of matter required to produce it. In the figure below, we can see that between 1990 and 2010 the US have consumed less and less domestic raw materials, which gives the impression of a decoupling between GDP and used resources.

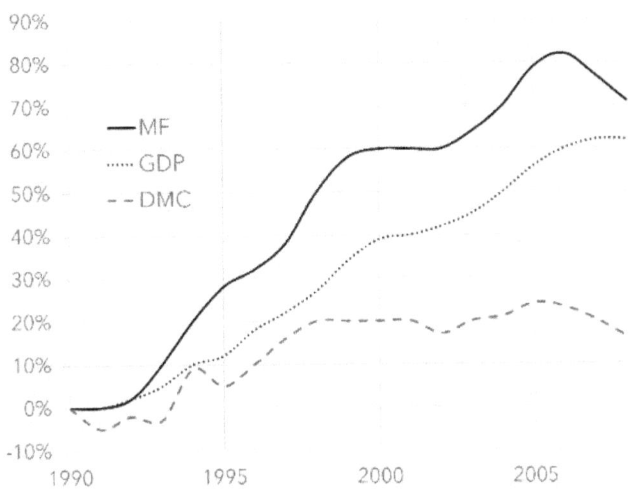

Figure 2.8 Total amount of raw materials (MF) used by the US production system (GDP) compared to domestic raw materials (DMC)

However, as soon as we include imported gross materials (that is, their total amount before waste), we can see that a real decoupling is still far out of reach.

Despite this fact, and although a full digital transformation has not yet been completed in any country, we can certainly say that advanced economies have all already entered the world of services. This trend is general, but it is more noticeable in the US economy.

2017	GDP (PPP $Mil)	Agriculture	Industry	Services
World	127.800.000	6,4%	30,0%	63.6%
Europe	20.850.000	1,6%	25,1%	70,9%
USA	19.490.000	0,9%	19,1%	80,0%

Table 2.3 Distribution of GDP by sector at Purchasing Power Parity (PPP)

As economies develop, the service sector always grows (health care, education, media, consulting firms, financial services etc...). At one point, and this is starting to happen right now, products themselves begin to transform into services, because it is the only way to ensure further sustainable growth. In the last two centuries, the US service sector has been steadily increasing (figure 2.9) and has been employing more and more people (figure 2.3).

Everywhere in the world, the importance of services is now well understood, but this idea is not yet being applied to industrial production; still, it is the only way to thrive while reducing the waste of materials and pollution.

The use of vast resources does not necessarily provide added value, nor does it significantly increase well-being. What happens instead is that sustainability problems increase out of all proportion.

The transition from product to service is fundamental, because it can steer us away from the socio-economic collapse predicted by the BAU scenario of the 'Limits to Growth' simulation.

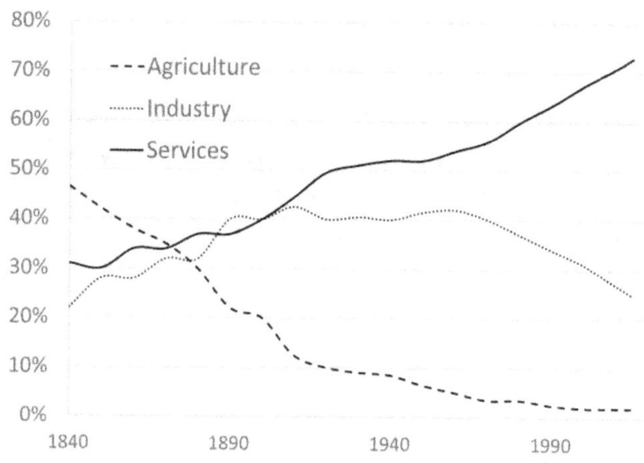

Figure 2.9 Trend of the three sectors from 1840 to 2015, in percentage of US GDP [67]

---

[67] Data sources: see note of Figure 2.3

In a nutshell, while the cowboy economy is based on tangible assets (consumption and repeated purchase of materials and products), the spaceman economy thrives in the world of the intangible, the only one where decoupling is possible.

In the spaceman economy, we can aim for growth without waste of resources and with a lower environmental impact. The traditional industrial model, based on the coupling of GDP growth with resource consumption, is now close to collapse; the decoupled mode is based on sustainability, with the consequence that, for the first time in human history, economies, societies and the ecology can all benefit from it.

The new model of digital production will therefore take us, again quoting Stahel, from "doing things right" to "doing the right things"[68].

2.5 Data is the new raw material

The Fourth Industrial Revolution brings out the value of data as a raw material. Thanks to software standardization, it is now easier than ever to develop new software applications, to create new information and new knowledge and, above all, to imagine new business models.

You may have heard the expression "data is the new oil", and that's exactly what it is: the more data we have, the more value we can extract from it. In the economy of matter, value is generated by scarcity; in the economy of data, value is generated by abundance.

Software - and especially Artificial Intelligence - needs data and at the same time produces new data: the difficulty lies in extracting value from the data itself. One of the best ways to extract value from data is to use it to implement a more

---

[68] *Ibid.*, Stahel W.R., *The Performance Economy*

profitable business model. Let's start from a fundamental notion.

We can think of data as a continuous sequence of symbols that must be transformed into information, that is, organized into understandable sequences with an unambiguous meaning. Data needs to be contextualized, that is, placed into a context that gives it meaning: the more detailed the context, the higher the value of the information that can be extracted.

For example, a thermostat in our home can tell us that the temperature is 71°F. This information is useful for an immediate use but does not carry a long-term value. If we consider this data without its context, it gives us very little information. If, on the other hand, we associate it with a specific context, we obtain much more information, for instance, that this temperature is measured in a specific geographical location, on a certain day of the year and at a certain time, that the heated room is located on the second floor with northern exposure and is used as a kitchen, and so on. More context increases the amount of information we can extract from data, and consequently its value.

Marketers know how important and valuable customer profiles are. Why shouldn't the same be true for object profiles that indirectly tell us about people, their environment, and their lifestyle habits? Knowing where and how an object is used is essential for making trend forecasts, but this contextualization of data would have been unthinkable in the past: if it is possible today, it is only thanks to the most recent developments of the IoT.

Before continuing, I would like to dwell on a very important concept, which is fundamental to understanding the scenario we are proposing: information is a physical quantity. Rolf Landauer, a researcher at IBM, postulated this concept in 1961[69].

Although the topic is controversial, the prevailing opinion is that information has for all intents and purposes physical characteristics. I like to think that information (information and computation) is a sort of "fifth element" that allows multiple combinations of the four physical quantities *par excellence*: matter, energy, space and time.

Until not so long ago, the nature of things was defined by these four quantities. As information progressively became an intrinsic component of things and their production, it became possible to use less matter, time, space and energy to obtain the same result.

It is precisely from this compression that innovation is generated.

This is crucial: information (processed by computers) allows the development of products that require less matter, time, space and energy to provide the same outcome.

Just like Buckminster Fuller[70] had predicted, thanks to technological progress we will be able to do more and more with less and less until, paradoxically, we will do everything with nothing. It is as if the four quantities of matter, energy, space and time were interchangeable with information and computation.

Information has also a central role in the life of all living organisms. Looking for information and making sense of it is an activity in which humans and animals are constantly engaged.

---

[69] Landauer R., *Information is Physical*, Physics Today, American Institute of Physics, May 1961

[70] *Ibid.*, Buckminster Fuller R., *Nine Chains to the Moon*

The search for information seems to be intrinsic to evolution itself: it is so relevant for the survival of living beings that it has been compared to food foraging[71].

In a work of 1983, George Miller uses for the first time the term 'informavore' to define higher living organisms: "In *What is life?*[72], a little book that opened up biology for physicists, Erwin Schrödinger pointed out that organisms survive by ingesting, not food, not calories, but negative entropy.

It is no accident, of course, that the mathematics of entropy are also the mathematics of information. The analogy is obvious: just as the body survives by ingesting negative entropy, so the mind survives by ingesting information.

In a very general sense, *all higher organisms are informavores.*"[73] We could therefore say that all technologies that help produce and collect information are favored, because they go in the right evolutionary direction.

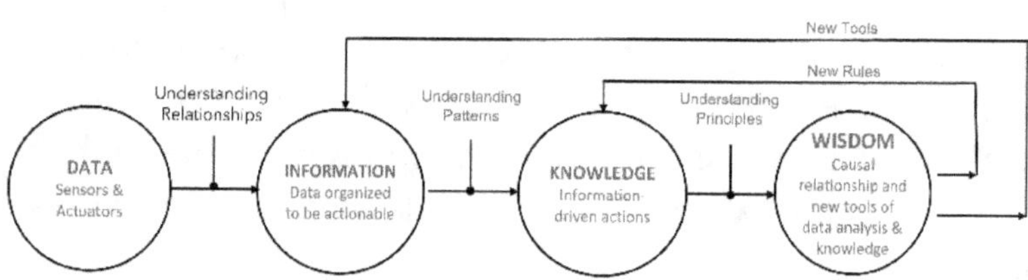

Figure 2.10 From data to knowledge: the life cycle of information

---

[71] Pirolli P., *Information Foraging Theory: Adaptive Interaction with Information*, Oxford University Press, New York 2007

[72] Schrödinger E., *What is Life? The Physical Aspect of the Living Cell*, University Press, Cambridge 1944

[73] Miller G., *Informavores*, in The Study of Information, F. Machlup and U. Mansfield (eds), Wiley 1983

The life cycle of information described in figure 2.10 is as follows: data is collected and organized into information, then transformed into knowledge by conventional algorithm-based software programs or by Artificial Intelligence programs.

In turn, this knowledge makes it possible to understand how certain phenomena or processes work, and more importantly, to make decisions accordingly.

In the above example of the room temperature, we could associate data coming from the thermostat with data related to the environment or to power consumption and assess how well or poorly insulated the house is.

Should the temperature rise to an unusual 120°F level, we could infer that some abnormal event is taking place in the house, such as the start of a fire.

By adding geolocation data to the context, we could intervene by contacting the owners or reaching the site with a rescue team. Needless to say, the same set of contextualized information can give rise to different types of knowledge, depending on the type of analysis performed.

Whenever possible, that is, technically and economically feasible, data should be stored in its 'native' form, reducing manipulations to a minimum so as not to lose information that might be necessary in case of future and different elaborations.

We should always remember that every transformation process applied to data potentially causes loss of information: there is a lot of knowledge hidden in what appears to be noise, because that noise holds other types of information that we are not yet able to decode.

The above considerations should be the basis of any IoT architecture implementation.

2.6 From M2M to the IoT

We are in the first stages of a great transition: we are shifting from the old industrial production mode to a new one driven by digitization. This shift will not be an easy one, given the impact it will have on all businesses. For some it may represent the end, for others it may be an opportunity for growth, and there will certainly be room for the creation of many new companies.

Digital technology is an enabling factor for the transition to a new economy, but nothing of the kind would be possible if the underlying ICT architecture had not evolved accordingly.

Over time, digital technologies have changed and improved. The hardware sector has taken the first big leaps and the software sector has followed suit, triggering a virtuous co-evolution that has brought us up to the present day.

Almost since their origin, computers have been connected to other objects, interfaces such as printers, terminals, external storage units and many others. These connections have always been partly bidirectional, but the interfaces were large, heavy and expensive.

Slowly, with the reduction of costs and dimensions and the development of both wired and wireless communication channels, computers have become so small and inexpensive as to be embedded into the objects themselves.

The acronym M2M (Machine to Machine) was used to indicate the first forms of data exchange between things with the help of integrated sensors, actuators and microelectronics.

These early connection methods were neither designed to collect real time data nor to extract value from data. Data was only functional to a specific application and was not exportable to other contexts. As the application using the data only worked in one particular context, there was no need for contextualization.

Going back to the example of the thermostat, we just needed the temperature. In short, data was not expected to have any value outside of the specific application for which it was required.

Besides, in M2M applications real time was not a strict constraint; many applications worked in the so-called *batch* mode, namely, data was collected over a period of time and sent to the central program only once a day, usually in the evening, so that the other software applications could have time to digest the new data overnight.

The first forerunners of the Internet of Things were born long before the Internet, when wireless telephony and Wi-Fi networks still did not exist, which means that they had to face very high computation and communication costs.

As far back as the seventies you could find them at Xerox Park, where Alan Key and Mark Weiser worked, and in the second half of the eighties at MIT's Media Lab, where Michael Hawley and Neil Gershenfeld worked. Although the term 'Internet of Things' was only coined in 1999 by British engineer Kevin Ashton, the pioneering work in the field of pervasive and ubiquitous computing done at Xerox Park and then at MIT's Media Lab already anticipated the interconnection of increasingly intelligent objects.

In the late eighties and early nineties, Mark Weiser - then a scientist at the Palo Alto Research Center in California - imagined a scenario that he very effectively outlined in three statements from his well-known article 'The Computer for the 21st Century'[74]:

---

[74] Weiser M., *The Computer for the 21st Century*, in Scientific American, Sept. 1991

The most profound technologies are those that disappear. They weave themselves into the fabric of everyday life until they are indistinguishable from it.

Like the wires in the walls, these hundreds of computers will come to be invisible to common awareness. People will simply use them unconsciously to accomplish everyday tasks.

Only when things disappear in this way are we freed to use them without thinking and so to focus beyond them on new goals.

In a presentation entitled "Internet of Things", Ashton, who was then working at a major cosmetics company, imagined an interesting scenario, which was already in Weiser's vision and in the writings of Hawley and Gershenfeld (the latter is the author of the book "When Things Start to Think"[75] from which Ashton drew inspiration).

Ashton's presentation suggested a possible solution to the problem of product tracking. At that time, the tracking was based on a barcode system, still in use today, that followed the product in its journey from one store to the other.

Unfortunately, the barcode could only reveal the product's presence in the store, not its location, so there was no way to know whether it was in the warehouse or on the shelf. Ashton's idea was to look at the problem from a different angle: by equipping each product with an RFID (Radio-Frequency IDentification) transponder, the products themselves would autonomously declare their position at any time.

The practical case that inspired this new methodology was a very popular lipstick which, although abundant in the warehouses, was always out of stock on the shelves. With the IoT approach, the shelf and the lipstick would be able to

---

[75] Gershenfeld N., *When Things Start to Think*, Henry Holt & Co., New York 1999

communicate, as would the lipstick and the warehouse, and so on.

As of today, more than two decades later, still not every product has an RFID transponder, and I wouldn't be able to say how many stores have smart shelves and implement the solution illustrated by Ashton.

IoT applications have only taken off on a somewhat large scale after 2015, although we expect a big acceleration in the present decade. For now, they are used more in consumer than in industrial settings, but the impending paradigm shift will force their adoption at a quick pace, as can be inferred from estimates of expected data generation.

This relatively simple example proves on one side, that non-real-time information is useless, and on the other side, that connectivity can be a feature of any physical object. Besides, the approach to data collection is changing; data are now enriched with their context and are used by several applications at the same time. In other words, data prevails over applications, and this multiplies the possibilities of use.

For our purposes, the two terms M2M and IoT are not interchangeable; however, we can consider the M2M architecture as a precursor to IoT. Incidentally, Ashton invented the term "Internet of Things" and gave an example of how it could be used but said nothing about the structure of the underlying computing architecture.

The IoT would remain only theoretical for many years to come, until with the advent of cellular connectivity, Cloud Computing and non-relational databases (which are at the heart of social networks) we were finally able to design and implement a low-cost scalable IoT architecture.

For a long time, interconnected systems have been developed with expensive technologies that were available only to a few companies and that certainly didn't allow for large-scale industrial adoption.

By contrast, today an IoT application is within the reach of almost any company, but the obstacle lies in the inability to generate value from collected data and in the risks related to cybersecurity, an issue that would deserve a whole book to itself but that we will not discuss here.

To conclude, we can say that IoT focuses on data and its accessibility, while M2M is based on a software application that knows the context and only receives strictly essential information. In our temperature example, an application for temperature control will only collect this value. All context-related data (time, date, geographic location etc.) will not be captured, and a predefined time and location will simply be allocated to the temperature values.

This data collection mode is extremely fast and efficient but has the side effect of creating a so-called 'data silos', a huge reservoir of data devoid of information relating to the context. Later, it will hardly be possible to reuse the same data in other applications, both because of the difficulty of extracting it from the silos, and because, even when successfully extracted, the data will still be without context.

Here the IoT opens up a new perspective. Thanks to the most recent technological advances, processing and storing large amounts of contextualized data is now not only possible, but also cost-effective.

As we can see in figure 2.11, the cost barrier that prevented data from being enriched with context information has been overcome.

Now we can store everything in a detailed and exhaustive manner, thereby giving collected data a lasting value, a value that goes beyond the application that is currently using it.

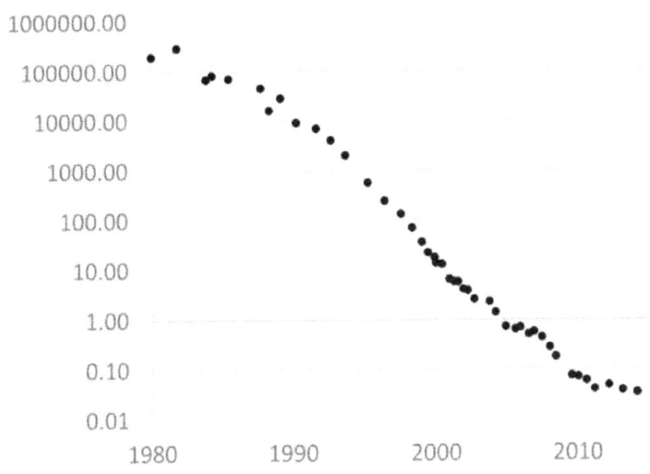

Figure 2.11 Cost per Megabyte of mass storage units (hard drives): from $200,000 in 1980 to $0.025 in 2015[76]

The concept of data silos is slowly being replaced by the concept of data lake: a vast pool of data that is rich in context but neutral with regard to applications.

All this is made possible by new computer architectures that provide one single tool to handle data collection, data distribution and data storage, while data processing is handed over to the application layer: a modular architecture consisting of loosely coupled subsystems, according to Simon's rule for complexity management.

2.7 Digital twins and the Metaverse

With the IoT, we are entering a new world of smart, collaborative objects. Objects are smart because they incorporate small, inexpensive and lightweight processors, and they are collaborative thanks both to wireless communications, which provide instant connection, and to

---

[76] Scher R., *Leveling the Playing Field*, Rowman & Littlefield, Guilford CT 2016

the evolution of software specifically implemented for the IoT.

Compared to traditional objects, smart objects have a life of their own: they can memorize events, respond to the context and communicate via the Internet.

When data gathered from smart objects is sent to the Cloud, a digital copy of the object is formed there, which is called a digital twin. This replica will be more or less accurate depending on the accuracy of the information sent to the Cloud by the object, and on the frequency with which the information is updated.

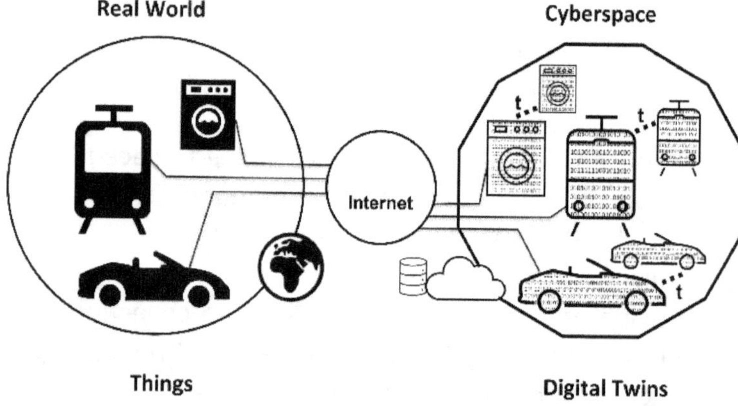

Figure 2.12 The digital twin: every 'thing' in the physical world will have a digital replica in the digital world

A digital twin is therefore a digital replica of a physical thing, inclusive of its context, created in real time by the IoT.

Note that this replica is not a simple virtual scan of a real object; it includes all the real time dynamics coming from live data feeds, plus all the collected data from the object's past.

This digital replica is made available to software applications through an appropriate messaging system, and is stored in the data lake, which is, as we said before, a specific database containing all the digital twins.

Suppose we have a smart thermostat connected to the Cloud. If we want to regulate a room's temperature, we only need to know the actual temperature and the desired temperature. But if we want to know the average temperature of all the houses in our neighborhood, it is much more convenient to store all the temperature data, with associated time and geographical position, in a data lake.

In this case, the digital twin of our thermostat does not only contain temperature data; it also contains all the surrounding data defining the context for each temperature.

With all this information accessible in the data lake, we can easily calculate the average temperature in the houses of our neighborhood, *even though* we did not think we might need it when we started collecting the data. Similarly, we could derive other types of information from the same data.

At the time of the Third Industrial Revolution, no one was interested in digital twins: data was stored without context, and no one thought that the same data could be used for a different purpose in the future. Today the exact opposite is true.

Even if we know exactly how to use data coming from things, we are aware that the value of this knowledge is limited to the here and now.

The future is unpredictable; tomorrow we may be required to treat data in new and different ways, and this is why we need to create replicas of all physical objects.

Like in T.S. Eliot's poem 'Burnt Norton', past, present and future become one:

Time present and time past
are both perhaps present in time future,
and time future contained in time past.

If all time is eternally present
all time is unredeemable.
What might have been is an abstraction
remaining a perpetual possibility
only in a world of speculation.
What might have been and what has been
point to one end, which is always present.[77]

A data lake stores both the real time data and all the historical data of an object, which allows accurate simulations of the object's behavior and short-term predictions on maintenance requirements and potential problems, keeping assets always in good operating conditions.

We can say, with Giarini[78], that the availability of all this information helps reduce the uncertainty that is intrinsic to the service economy model.

Digital twins also provide a more agile approach to programming, because an increasing number of applications can use the same data in different contexts and for different purposes. As we said, the main focus is on data, and software is eating everything.

This new reality requires servitized products to be in perfect operating condition, and this means access to real time data or, in other words, digital twins.

Without digital twins it is impossible to keep things under control, and it is therefore impossible to generate new services. In the case of a self-driving car, for instance, it is not enough for the car to be able to drive itself.

We also need to know in real time where it is and what the surrounding conditions are, not only to plan its optimal use, but also to be able to act promptly should anomalies arise.

---

[77] Eliot T.S., *Burnt Norton* in *Four Quartets*, Faber and Faber, London 1940-42
[78] *Ibid.*, Giarini O., Stahel W.R., *The Limits to Certainty*

Needless to say, these two aspects are both essential to ensure an adequate and reassuring customer experience.

It is also possible to create digital twins of objects and machines that were built during the First, Second and Third Industrial Revolutions, before the birth of the IoT. These objects, which do not have electronics parts, or have only electronic parts not connected to the Internet, are collectively called 'brown-field' devices.

Other more recent objects, born during the Fourth Industrial Revolution, are connected from the start; they are collectively called 'green-field' devices.

A green-field machine is already equipped with sensors, software applications and a built-in Internet connection that make its digital twin natively available.

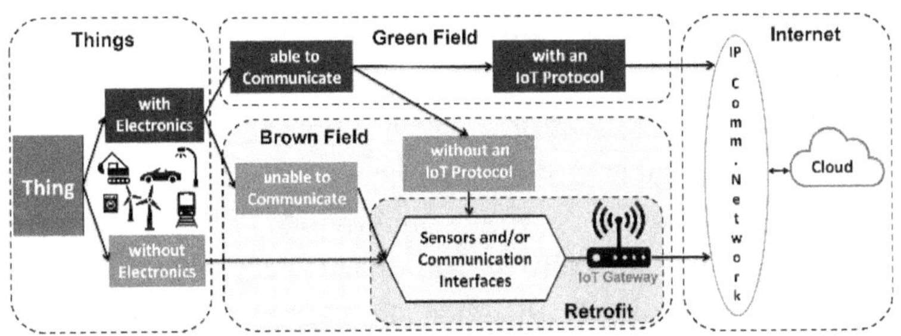

Figure 2.13 Connecting brown-field and green-field devices to the Internet

The great majority of industrial machines in operation today are not connected; in order to enter the digital world, they need a retrofit, which will be discussed in Part IV.

Retrofitting is often necessary because companies are not willing to get rid of old machines, especially when the cost has already been fully amortized and the production efficiency is still high.

To update these machines, it is often enough to add sensors that return the operating status if the machine is mechanical or electromechanical, or to add a communication system plus some sensors if it is equipped with electronics. This retrofit, now available thanks to technology, gives companies an opportunity to revitalize existing plants and old machines without making major investments.

Although the resulting digital twins will not always be very precise, they will be reliable enough to allow these machines to perform their task for many years to come.

We cannot talk about the IoT and digital twins without mentioning the Metaverse, which is a direct consequence of their existence. If the data lake is the place where apps can digitally access digital twins, then the Metaverse is the place where humans can virtually interact with digital twins.

The word 'Metaverse' dates back to 1992, when it was used for the first time by Neal Stephenson in his novel 'Snow Crash'[79] to describe an immersive virtual reality.

Since then, the word's meaning has evolved to signify a combination of the physical world with the virtual world. A good definition of it is the following:

"The Metaverse is the convergence of 1) virtually-enhanced physical reality and 2) physically-persistent virtual space. It is a fusion of both, while allowing users to experience it as either"[80].

Clearly, digital twins are essential to the Metaverse. We could say that they constitute a sort of Metaverse in themselves: "The Metaverse will be the place where IoT digital twins will come together to party"[81].

The Metaverse in itself is simply a cybernetic space which contains both virtual objects and virtual replicas of real

---

[79] Stephenson N., *Snow Crash*, Bantam Books, New York 1992
[80] Smart J., Cascio J., Paffendorf J., https://www.metaverseroadmap.org/overview/
[81] Schouw B., https://blog.softwareag.com/iot-digital-twins-metaverse

objects, i.e. digital twins. What makes it really interesting is that humans can access the Metaverse, either by entering a completely virtual fantasy world like a videogame, or by interacting with a virtual world that simulates the real world through digital twins.

Although some kind of virtual reality has been accessible for some time now, this access has mostly been difficult and expensive.

The fact that digital technologies (smart glasses, haptic interfaces, smartphones, computers etc.) have become exponentially more efficient while their cost has vastly decreased opens up the possibility of an easy interaction between the two worlds, which finally makes the Metaverse a 'reality'.

In the Metaverse, information and interactions go both ways: any action performed in one world can produce changes in the other. For instance, the additional audio and video information coming from the cyberspace gives humans an amplified representation of reality which helps them better understand and improve the physical world.

Physical reality changes virtual reality because the sensors located on real objects send data which immediately modifies their digital twins. Similarly, virtual reality changes physical reality because the actuators located on real objects receive commands from their digital twins which immediately modify the real world, unless this is prevented for some reason; for instance, if we are simulating critical conditions, we want the results of the simulation to remain in the virtual world.

As we have seen, in the Metaverse reality merges with virtuality to create an amplified perception of the real world. This allows more precise and efficient decision-making, which is a big accelerating factor for digitization and for business transformation: it will provide companies with detailed answers to 'what-if' questions and with the ability to derive insights from massively complex environments, something that would be impossible to achieve by monitoring the physical environment alone.

Many things can be done from the Metaverse using digital twins. The Metaverse makes it possible not only to reproduce reality but also to perform really complex simulations, like predicting the behavior of an autonomous car in predefined conditions of weather or traffic, on a specific route and with different kinds of other vehicles on the road.

From the Metaverse, we can remotely maneuver robots or simulate the behavior of objects in the design phase; for instance, the digital twin of a bridge or a skyscraper can be put in a virtual flood or virtual earthquake situation to highlight weaknesses and improve design.

However, the greatest value of digital twins lies in the fact that they help control operational risk by preventing potentially dangerous situations, namely, by allowing programs to block the actuators in the real objects before errors and failures occur.

In a virtual simulation, digital twins behave and operate exactly how they would in the real world. The insights obtained from the simulated digital twin can then be applied to the real twin back in the physical environment, with tremendous benefits in terms of short-term behavior prediction.

Needless to say, this predictive capacity is an indispensable tool that will allow business models based on servitization to become pervasive and transformative in all sectors.

PART III

From the IoT to the outcome economy

*If an industrial society is defined by the quantity of goods
as marking a standard of living, the post-industrial society
is defined by the quality of life
as measured by the services and amenities
—health, education, recreation, and the arts—
which are now deemed desirable and possible for everyone.*

Daniel Bell

3.1 The long path to an Industrial IoT architecture

In the first two Parts I have focused on the development of digital technologies and on their fundamental contribution to the emergence of a new production mode. Within this framework, I hope I have been able to convey the importance of data and, above all, the importance of collecting data in real time and in context, so that it can be easily stored, retrieved and reused. Behind this sophisticated mode of data collection and management there is one single fundamental technology: the IoT computing architecture.

Thanks to the IoT, lots of data are being collected and stored, and digital twins are beginning to take shape. The same IoT, by generating huge amounts of data that must be managed, is inspiring the growth of Artificial Intelligence.

However, despite its importance, the path to this essential computing architecture has not been linear or obvious. My professional experience, which I now have the pleasure to share with you, testifies to how the IoT has slowly taken shape, progressively evolving over time.

The route to the IoT had already been traced by Mark Weiser's research in the late eighties; Weiser used the expression 'ubiquitous computing' (ubicomp) to indicate the gradual transformation of passive objects into 'smart things', that is, things with a computer inside, i.e. an embedded computer.

At the time, some smart things were already collecting information from their surroundings and exchanging data, but the focus was not on data; it was essentially on hardware devices and on some software applications: data was still 'trapped' within the applications.

Although the overall design was clear, something was still missing. The body, so to say, was already well defined in its external form and function, but the backbone to support it and make it stand upright was not there yet: what was missing was a modern IoT architecture.

As a matter of fact, the concept behind the IoT already existed, but it was not clear how this scenario could be implemented on an industrial scale. Mark Weiser himself was well aware that the technologies of the time were still inadequate to make his ubicomp vision come true, and he said so in one of his most famous articles[82].

It took another twenty years for Weiser's vision to become a reality. This reality is the IoT.

Back in the nineties, the idea that the objects around us would gradually become intelligent, and that they would communicate with each other and with human beings, already seemed quite natural to me, but at the time we had to deal with other problems: the size and power consumption of computers were such that they could not be incorporated into everyday objects.

There was still a lot of work to be done on the hardware side, in terms of minimizing dimensions and lowering power consumption. In fact, this hurdle prevented me from thinking about the possible evolutions of software.

Computers were slowly beginning to literally get 'inside' things, but these tiny computers did not communicate at a distance, they did not share data, they interacted only locally and not necessarily with other computers. We were still far from Mark Weiser's vision of ubiquitous or pervasive computing.

---

[82] *Ibid.*, Weiser M., *The Computer for the 21st Century*

In the late nineties Louis Gerstner, at the time CEO of IBM, foresaw that pervasive computing would be our future. He declared:

"Someday soon, more than one million businesses will be connected to more than one billion people by one trillion devices. It's already beginning to happen with these new 'Net access' devices like intelligent screen phones and intelligent smart cards. But we'll see even more tremendous growth when intelligence becomes embedded, when virtually everything becomes a computing device. Technology will disappear into the very fabric of everything we do. It will be embedded in cars, your tools, in your homes, your school, and your workplace. Applications and services will be delivered much in the manner that a utility company provides electricity or water today."[83]

For me, this was an indication that, ten years after Mark Weiser's work, the notion of ubiquitous or pervasive computing was beginning to move out of the labs and into the economy. Gerstner was giving economic viability to Mark Weiser's technological vision: he was predicting the emergence of digital services delivered automatically by computers. At that exact moment in history, the concept of adding value to a product by combining it with one or more services was born. Still, the idea of a complete transition from product to service had not yet been fully entertained, at least by me.

The first smartphones would appear only some years later, and social networks were still far down the line. At that time everyone was fixated on Grid Computing, and investigating

---

[83] https://www.industryweek.com/leadership/companies-executives/article/21963777/driving-success-at-new-blue

ways to write applications that used distributed and connected computers.

In hindsight I know that we should have reversed our thinking: instead of asking ourselves how the applications could use the computer Grid, we should have asked how the computer Grid could serve the applications.

The concept of the Cloud was still a long way off, but it is interesting to note that the difference between the Grid and the Cloud is in the word 'service'.

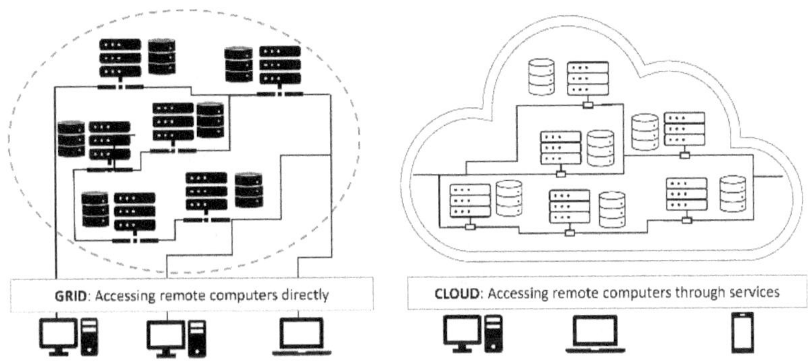

Figure 3.1 From Grid Computing to Cloud Computing

Here again, in order to make a quantum leap in the use of distributed computing resources, servitization is the key. Basically, from a hardware standpoint the Grid and the Cloud are the same thing, that is, clusters of interconnected and distributed computers. The difference lies in how they can be accessed, meaning the difference lies in the software.

By the year 2000, in compliance with Moore's law, computers had reached such small dimensions and such low consumption and cost that the ubicomp vision could finally become a reality. In this context, my impression was that once the hardware problems were solved, the software would naturally evolve to accommodate the trend toward pervasive computing.

Actually, this transition did not come easily: a big paradigm shift was needed, a surprising innovation like the well-known 'Fosbury flop'.

After 2005 it became clear to me that things were not going as expected. Software was struggling to keep up with the ubiquitous computing mode, and as a result all hardware improvements were useless: we desperately needed new software tools.

We could no longer think of the operating system as the backbone upon which all software applications were developed. Nor could we continue to think in terms of Grid Computing, that is, of distributed computing and storage resources.

We had to change our way of thinking; the answer was right under our nose, but we couldn't see it. I sensed that the solution had to do with data, that data would somehow become the new center of gravity. I assumed that data would have to be kept somewhere, in a sort of large database that would store all the data coming from smart objects, regardless of who the end user might be.

At the time I was imagining a massive data collection platform, but it was just an intuition and I wasn't clear on how it could be implemented. It was a primitive idea of decoupling to manage complexity, suggested by Herbert Simon's theory of complex systems (see Part I). Based on Simon's idea of loosely coupled subsystems, one could imagine a two-subsystems solution: a basic subsystem that would collect data from things, and a platform subsystem where data would be made available to all possible applications.

It was a bit like what had happened with freight logistics. In the past, each manufacturer had his own fleet of trucks.

Then, express couriers began to offer dedicated transport services: goods were collected and sorted, then taken to a large hub used as a buffer warehouse.

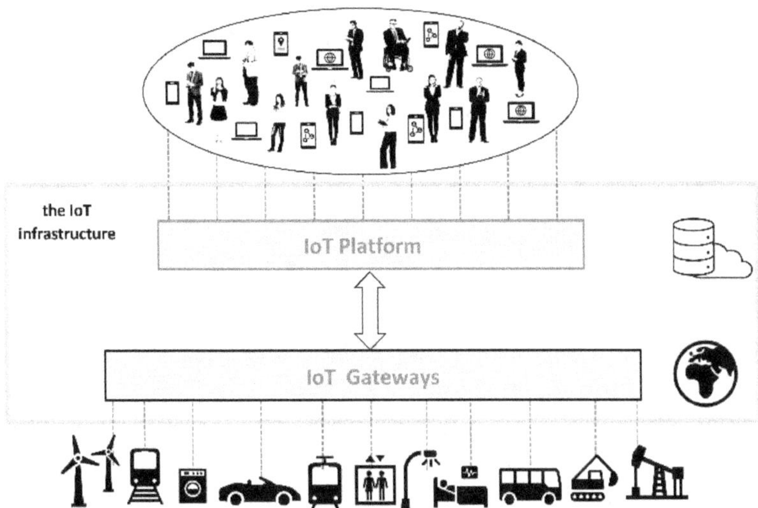

Figure 3.2 The IoT infrastructure and the two main subsystems: the IoT gateways close to 'things' and the IoT Platform in the Cloud

Similarly, data could also use a dedicated transport service: computers at the periphery would collect and sort data, then send it to a central platform, a hub of computers managing the database.

To tell the truth, around 2007 the first faint signs of a new reality were already visible, but they were somewhere else. To notice them, I should have looked in another direction, and it was not an easy thing to do: a new animal was taking shape, and I only had a glimpse of its tail and paws.

Seeing the new animal is always difficult because we tend to imagine a familiar shape, while in fact it is a completely different creature. In this specific case, I should have looked at the new world of mobile telephony with smartphones and apps, where Cloud Computing architecture would soon reveal all its disruptive power.

The Cloud was actually born for a different purpose, as a means to increase computing and storage resources without major software reprogramming or reconfigurations. Basically, the original goal was to quickly improve the efficiency of the IT infrastructure as the demand for computing and storage resources grew, for example due to a rapid increase in customers and purchases on e-commerce sites.

It is no coincidence that the Cloud was born with Amazon in 2006, even though the concept of computers as utilities had been theorized much earlier, by John McCarthy (one of the fathers of Artificial Intelligence along with Simon), in his 1961 MIT Centennial speech:

"If computers of the kind I have advocated become the computers of the future, then computation may someday be organized as a public utility, just as the telephone system is a public utility. We can envisage computing service companies whose subscribers are connected to them by telephone lines. Each subscriber needs to pay only for the capacity that he actually uses, but he has access to all programming languages characteristic of a very large system. The system could develop commercially in fairly interesting ways. Certain subscribers may offer services to other subscribers"[84].

The concept of Software-as-a-Service (SaaS), a software that can be made available through the Internet and the browser without the need for complicated installations on the computer, was developed at the end of the nineties, but it gained momentum only with the emergence of Cloud Computing. Before the Cloud, companies had to invest

---

[84] McCarthy J., *Time-Sharing Computer Systems* in Management and the Computer of the Future, M. Greenberger Ed., The MIT Press, Cambridge MA 1962

heavily in building their own computing infrastructure, the so-called data center, and ended up with a rigid structure that was very difficult to change or improve later on.

Furthermore, this lack of flexibility regularly led companies to build data centers that were oversized and more expensive than needed. In 2000, when things went awry with the so-called 'Internet bubble', this meant a huge loss of resources and dramatic bankruptcies.

With the advent of the Cloud, the data center infrastructure becomes a pay-per-use service: companies can choose its size and power, and change their requirements as needed. If a similar crisis took place today, companies would simply unsubscribe from the service, without having to dismantle highly technological installations and to waste costly assets.

I would like to share my personal experience to illustrate how hard it was to develop new products before Cloud Computing, and without software writing tools for distributed computers.

In 2000 we started to develop the Zypad, one of the first wearable computers in the world. Following the same software approach that is normally used for desktop computers and laptops, we installed an operating system, the Microsoft Windows CE, which was a reinterpretation of Windows for PDAs, pocket PCs and various other small low-power devices. The PDA (Personal Digital Assistant) was a kind of very powerful math calculator which also had some other functions (notebook, agenda, address book etc.) and a minimal wireless connectivity; it could be considered an early precursor of the smartphone, with a lot fewer features.

For easy handling, the PDA's screen was vertical, which is common today in smartphones but was very innovative for those times, and it did not have the automatic screen rotation function, because it lacked rotation sensors. At the time, no one thought of using the PDA horizontally and all the applications were programmed to be displayed vertically, as opposed to desktop applications that were instead programmed to be displayed horizontally.

For ergonomic reasons, in particular the need to read the screen while wearing the computer on the arm, the Zypad was designed with the same components used for PDAs, but with an horizontal screen.

Basically, we applied a desktop horizontal screen to a PDA architecture. We thought that our wearable computer Zypad could use all the applications developed for PDAs, but we were confronted with a huge problem: the applications were designed for a vertical screen and adapting them was almost impossible.

Few software companies were willing to rewrite all the code to adapt it to a horizontal screen... due to a simple portability issue, the Zypad project was abandoned. Although it may seem unbelievable today, such things did happen before smartphones and the app economy.

3.2 Behind the scenes of Apple's success

The true paradigm shift, the ultimate expression of the software revolution, manifested itself around 2010 with the loss of Nokia's leadership to Apple. Ever since iTunes, Apple had been aware that its strength lay not solely in the hardware but also in the availability of digital content.

After all, compared to Sony's digital Walkman, what did the iPod have to offer? From the point of view of hardware and sound, absolutely nothing. Yet, the iPod gave access to the iTunes digital store where you could buy music, even just one song at a time and not necessarily a whole music album.

Later, Apple applied the same logic to the iPhone project. Apple's iPhone was not just a phone, it was a system whose core was a platform that allowed developers to quickly create new applications and new multimedia content.

The development platform was associated with a service that made apps immediately marketable: the App Store. This platform system, which offered many advantages to all participants, both producers and consumers of content, was the trump card that sanctioned Apple's definitive victory over Nokia.

In my mind, however, something was still unclear: Apple's great success was evident and understandable, but the underlying structure puzzled me. How did these new platform systems really work? Apple had developed a platform where data producers and data consumers could converge.

I liked the idea of a platform as a kind of harbor where data could be exchanged like any other commodity, and which would operate according to a set of basic rules. Once these rules established, there would be no need to define specific rules for each device or app. Devices and apps would simply have to comply with the rules of the platform.

To better explain what follows and to avoid misconstructions, I would like to clarify the distinction between a software platform and a business platform.

A software platform is a set of software modules which have access to the system's resources and are used to simplify the writing of applications.

A business platform, on the other hand, is an infrastructure used to match the supply and demand of products.

Incidentally, a business platform will allow business models to grow, initially, in a linear, then quadratic, and hopefully exponential way, according to the laws discussed in Part I.

The exponential growth of a business platform can only be activated by software applications that introduce the possibility of creating subsets of users (Reed's law), for instance, social networks or digital marketplaces.

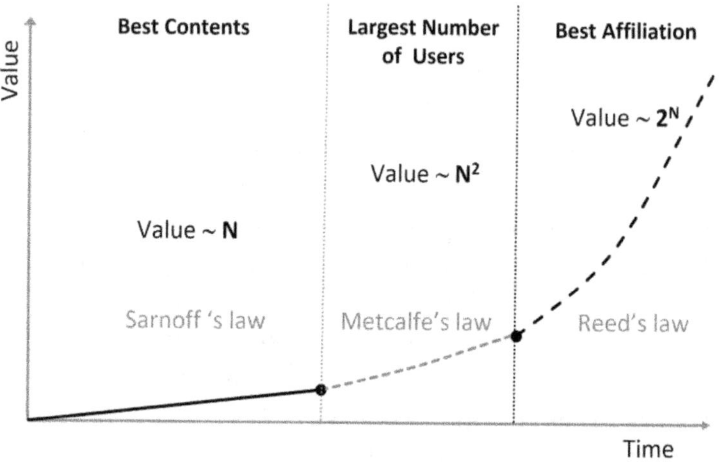

Figure 3.3 Growth of a business from linear to exponential

What I needed at the time was an innovative platform that had both the infrastructure of a business platform, to connect data producers (things) with data consumers (apps), and the features of a software platform, to speed up and simplify app development.

The system would constantly collect and update real-time data from a number of devices that could grow indefinitely.

At the heart of this system, I imagined a pool where all the data of connected things would be stored, either in an unstructured form or as digital twins. This kind of flexible data warehouse would later be called a data lake.

I continued to ponder this idea for some time, but I couldn't get a clear vision of it, until something finally happened. One evening that I won't forget I was in the marketing office, leafing absent-mindedly through a magazine, when I came across an image that caught my attention.

It was a drawing titled 'The Cloud', an upside-down pyramid divided into three layers. Suddenly, all the pieces of the puzzle fell into place.

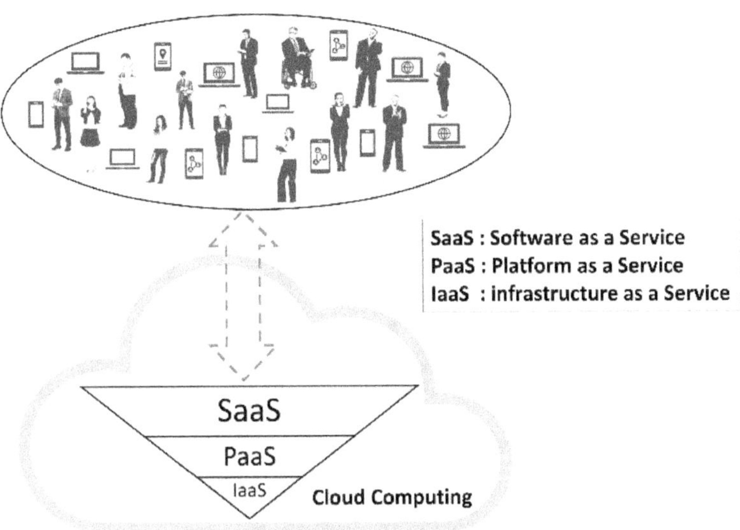

Figure 3.4 The Cloud's inverted pyramid

3.3 From things to people: the two pyramids

The image of the Cloud's pyramid gave me a clear and precise idea of the structure that was taking shape. In particular, it suggested a pattern that finally made perfect sense: below the Cloud's inverted pyramid, I imagined another pyramid, upright this time: the pyramid of smart things connected to the Internet.

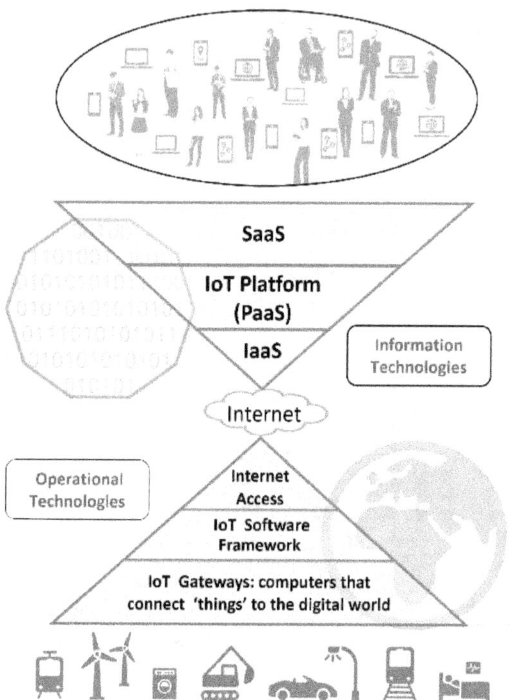

Figure 3.5 The two pyramids of the IoT architecture

Let's examine the drawing above, starting from the bottom. Below the base of the upright pyramid, we have all the things that need to be connected.

These objects are equipped with sensors and actuators that collect data from the environment and send it to the Cloud.

On the first level of the pyramid, we find a layer of computers which serve as gateways (bridges or interfaces between the real world and the digital world of the Cloud).

Incidentally, these particular computers can be called IoT gateways, IoT edge gateways or IoT edge computers, depending on their computing and storage capacity; for the sake of simplicity, I will refer to them as 'IoT gateways' from now on.

On the second level of the pyramid we have the Software Framework, a large set of software modules that can be used to manage the IoT gateways and to develop software applications for them. On the third level we have the communication interfaces that give access to the Internet.

The whole structure has the shape of an upright pyramid because the elements are fewer and simpler as we go up: at the base, a huge number of things, each one different from the others, and each requiring a specific physical interface; in the middle, a software framework which reduces the complexity of interface management; at the top, a very simple Internet connection.

Its counterpart in the Cloud is represented by an inverted pyramid with the tip at the bottom.

The first level consists of the physical infrastructure (computation, storage and Internet access) that is delivered as a service and is called IaaS (Infrastructure-as-a-Service).

The middle layer is populated by software platforms, including IoT platforms that provide easy access to the data collected by things; these platforms are also delivered as a service and are called PaaS (Platform-as-a-Service).

At the top, in the largest layer, we finally find all the applications, which are uncountable and extremely varied, and are also delivered as a service.

This third layer is called SaaS (Software-as-a-Service). The Cloud pyramid is upside-down because the quantity and scalability increase as we go up: on a few IaaS we can have a lot of PaaS, and on a lot of PaaS we can have countless SaaS.

To recap, we have broken down the IoT architecture into two pyramids, one of which is inverted. Each pyramid features three functional layers. The pyramid on top represents the IT (Information Technologies) side of the architecture, while the pyramid at the bottom represents the OT (Operational Technologies) side of the architecture. The two sides communicate through an Internet connection.

To explain how all of this works, we now have to introduce the APIs (Application Program Interfaces). APIs are calls to functions of the software platforms that can be compared to the library calls of the past.

For example, every time we launch the Facebook app from our smartphone, the app will use APIs to exchange data with the Facebook platform in the Cloud. In the bottom pyramid (OT side), we have the Software Framework layer which provides local APIs for writing applications on the IoT gateway located close to the things.

In the top pyramid (IT side) we have the IoT platform layer which provides APIs for writing applications in SaaS mode. As a result, we do not need to know in detail how the two pyramids work to write applications; we only need to know what to do with our data and how to access it through the APIs.

Here again, in accordance with Simon's theory[85], a complex system has been broken down into a number of loosely coupled subsystems (and I would like to add, connected by standard interfaces). This is exactly how we designed our IoT architecture and how the majority of IoT architectures are designed today.

Just so we don't overlook anything, I also want to point out that there are three types of Cloud: public, private and on premises. An IoT platform can be installed on any of these three Cloud types depending on the specific needs of the customer.

---

[85] *Ibid.*, Simon H.A., *The Architecture of Complexity*

In the public Cloud, both the infrastructure and the IoT platform are shared among all customers, who also share the infrastructure and management costs.

In the private Cloud, the infrastructure is still shared among all customers, but each customer has their own private IoT platform and pays for the related management costs.

As for the Cloud 'on premises', both the infrastructure, which is built at the customer's premises, and the IoT platform are reserved for that one customer. In this case, the customer pays both for the computers that make up the infrastructure and for the management of the IoT platform.

3.4 The spread of software services

To better understand the IoT, it might help to think of it as a kind of social network of things. If we look at it this way, we see that things, like humans, need a 'smartphone' to communicate on the Internet and to exchange data with other things.

The IoT gateway is just that: a smartphone for things where instead of a keyboard and video there is a program, and where data (temperature, humidity, acceleration...) comes from the sensors of things rather than from a human mind and senses.

Then, just like humans send their feedback over the Internet using a microphone and camera or a keyboard, things influence their surroundings using their actuators (motors, relays, valves...). To create and manage this social network of things, all we have to do is adopt the same software tools used in human social networks, just made suitable for industrial use.

In 2010 we finally had our own model for the realization of a massive platform for data collection and management - an

IoT platform - and at the beginning we thought of it as complementary to our hardware product, which was the IoT gateway.

The IoT platform, which drastically simplified software development, could have been made available to customers free of charge, to make the hardware product more attractive and more competitive. Even then, I was still unable to see that the IoT platform could change our business model.

Although I had been developing digital products for years, I was stuck in the industrial production mindset: I did not understand that the IoT could transform every hardware product into a service.

Only some time later did I realize that data could change everything and that it could help achieve the sustainable growth envisioned by Giarini and Stahel.

As I have already mentioned, in the digital production mode data is the new raw material: thanks to digital twins updated in real time, it is possible to replace the sale of products with the sale of their use or performance.

In our case, the IoT platform would turn into a data transport service, and customers would pay a subscription fee to use it. Some customers might prefer to have the software license and manage the service themselves, but in any case, they would still have to pay a subscription fee.

The reason was simple: even in the world of industrial software, which is very reluctant to upgrade, cybersecurity was breaking the rules of the past.

In today's connected world, cybersecurity cannot be ignored and requires constant software updates. In the past, companies that purchased computers and installed them on their machines - say, a metal lathe or a hydraulic press - were at no risk because neither the machine nor the computer were connected to the Internet.

As long as the software worked well for its purpose, there was no reason to upgrade it. Today things are very different because all these machines are connected: everyone constantly needs to update their software to make it immune to cyberattacks.

At the time our company was a computer hardware manufacturer, but the IoT and cybersecurity propelled us into the world of recurring revenue from services: we could ask for a subscription fee to provide secure data transport services and software update services.

Back to our Cloud pyramid, we can see that each layer, viewed as a service, includes the services of the layers below it.

Anything that includes a service can in turn become a service: the infrastructure is a service, the platform is a service that also includes the infrastructure service, the software application is a service that includes the platform service and the infrastructure service. Now we might wonder why the vast majority of apps are free of charge.

In a nutshell, when we use an application, we can be either data consumers or data prosumers, that is, producers and clients at the same time. In the first case the application cannot be provided for free and someone will pay for it, either directly or indirectly (through advertising).

In the second case, if in addition to consuming data we also produce some, the payment will be made indirectly in the form of data that we submit while using the app. Nothing is free, not even in the world of apps, but as they spread, and with advances in technology, management costs will go down, together with prices.

We are quickly approaching the so-called 'zero marginal cost' society, where the marginal cost of digital products and of their distribution (see Netflix, McAfee etc.) is getting so low that it is almost zero, provided that the initial costs have been covered and subscribers have reached a critical mass.

As we approach zero-cost computation, communication and storage, everything is going to be digitized; when everything is digitized, companies will realize that the servitization model is the most cost-effective one; besides, they will become aware that they can reduce operational risks thanks to the short-term predictions made possible by digital twins.

At this point, they will automatically transition to selling services.

3.5 Discovering the servitization paradigm

To illustrate the servitization paradigm, let's start with two questions. Assuming we manufacture devices that never break down, is it more profitable for us to sell them or to adopt a pay-per-use model? And to implement a pay-per-use model, what kind of technology do we need?

Many tools and devices today are already available for rental or leasing. Office photocopiers, for example, used to be purchased together with a good maintenance contract.

Now that copiers, thanks to technological improvements, don't break down anymore, manufacturers get almost no revenue from maintenance.

This is why they are adopting an outcome economy model where customers no longer buy the machine; they simply pay for the number of copies made. Turning a copy machine into a service is not that difficult in a digital and connected world. And since in large offices photocopiers sometimes disappear, indoor tracking techniques are being developed to track assets that are lost or displaced and end up missing, which is also a well-known problem in the field of health care equipment[86].

Other kinds of assets have always been provided as a service, for instance private and commercial housing, but thanks to advances in technology and to the improved quality of life, these traditional services are quickly evolving.

Today, renting out an office no longer means providing a certain space, but also assuring adequate climatic conditions, so that the people who use it can work comfortably. In a near future, not only will it be possible to create ideal climatic conditions, but also to maintain them over time through non-stop monitoring. In addition, energy consumption will be carefully tracked, allowing reliable predictions of future consumption. As we can see, once in place the service economy will quickly shift from selling a use to selling an outcome or a performance.

Nowadays, advanced climate control also provides information on the functioning of the heating or cooling system, allowing timely maintenance of the plants and even accurate prediction of impending failures. This is what we call predictive maintenance.

If the system has a digital twin, it will be easy to monitor the internal climate parameters of a building and to identify in advance the onset of a problem. It's a bit like what a doctor does by reading and interpreting data from blood tests, for example.

We are all aware of the importance of preventive medicine: regular check-ups can identify a disease at an early stage and treat it before it creates serious problems. The same principle can be applied to objects, machinery and

---

[86] https://www.sciedupress.com/journal/index.php/jha/article/view/10752

plants if they are properly sensorized, digitized and connected.

One of the most meaningful illustrations of the servitization paradigm is undoubtedly the self-driving car, because of its numerous practical implications. As we have seen, the large-scale transition from product to service strongly depends on the collection of real time data and on its storage.

This data makes it possible to constantly monitor the asset provided as a service and to predict its behavior in the short term. In the case of a car, we already have rental companies that provide the service, but they give you the car for no less than a day and with the condition of returning it where it was picked up, under penalty of a surcharge.

Why is this? The reason is that rental companies would face very high costs if they had to bring back the car from a distant location before renting it out again, and more important, they would be unable to assess any damage suffered by the car during its use. In other words, providing a car when users need it, just for the time they need it, and allowing them to leave it where it best suits them, is not a viable business model for the time being.

This business model would become sustainable if the car was always connected and self-driving. The service offered by Uber is a bit like that, with the only difference that the driver is a special kind of supercomputer equipped with sophisticated sensors and actuators: a human being.

In fact, we can consider Uber's business model as a precursor of car use as an alternative to car ownership. By the time driverless cars become a reality, Uber will be in a position of extreme competitive advantage, and its fares will probably be so low that owning a car will be disadvantageous. In the meantime, Uber collects the data it needs, and will need even more in the future, to efficiently deliver car services.

Even though Uber is not yet a profitable company and cannot be evaluated based on this indicator, it is nevertheless accumulating great value: its context-rich data. Data can be transformed into information, and information into knowledge on how to run the business.

Many car manufacturers are now investing resources in fully self-driving cars, not so much to keep selling cars but in view of changing their business model. There are six levels of car autonomy, numbered from 0 to 5, and they are described in the table below.

Level of Autonomy	Road Control	Type of Autonomy	Description	Example
L0	Human Driver	No automation	The driver drives and has supervision over the support functions	Emergency brake, blind spot detector, lane departure warning
L1	Human Driver	Assisted drive	The driver drives and has supervision over the support functions	Lane centering or adaptive cruise control
L2	Human Driver	Assisted drive Partial automation	The driver drives and has supervision over the support functions	Lane centering and adaptive cruise control
L3	Human Driver & Automation	Assisted drive Conditional automation	The driver does not drive when automation is in control of the car. The driver drives when required by automation	Autonomous driving in congested traffic situations
L4	Automated Pilot	High automation	Automation is in control of the car under certain defined conditions. There is no driver.	Taxi without driver. Pedals and steering can be optional
L5	Automated Pilot	Fully automated	Automation is in control of the car. There is no driver	Like level 4 but automation can drive autonomously in all conditions

Table 3.1 Car autonomy levels according to SAE (Society of Automobile Engineers)[87]

While there's no doubt that self-driving cars will be part of our everyday lives, it will be at least five years before they

---

[87] https://www.sae.org/news/press-room/2018/12/sae-international-releases-updated-visual-chart-for-its-%E2%80%9Clevels-of-driving-automation%E2%80%9D-standard-for-self-driving-vehicles

actually appear on the market. Currently, level 3 cars are marketable: they do almost everything autonomously, even if they require the presence of a human being who remains in charge.

Up to level 3, driving is simply made easier and less stressful, accidents are less frequent and, even when tired and sleepy, the driver can still make it home safe and sound.

This type of car is still a product to be sold and the business model does not change. At level 4, some specific services like city cabs start to be automated. Only at level 5 will cars be considered, even by the general public, as a real service and no longer as a product.

As cars get more autonomous, more and more data will accumulate, and will need to be transported and managed: the 5G network and its future evolutions will of course be essential. Totally autonomous cars will need extremely sophisticated communication technologies, hundred percent real-time, because they will have to talk to each other to decide how to behave in a myriad of situations.

Up to level 3 autonomy, cars can continue to be sold in the traditional way. At this level, those who buy cars don't do so because they distrust autonomous vehicles but simply because they like to drive the car themselves.

Going above level 3 means applying totally different business models with progressive servitization. At level 5, for instance, a large number of services will be provided directly in the cabin, because driving will no longer require any attention.

With autonomous cars, the big problem of sustainability will finally be solved: as it is today, a car is used on average, on a global basis, for about 4% of the time of ownership, which means that the car is parked on the street or in the garage for a striking 96% of the time, a huge waste of matter that remains immobilized and unavailable.

We all know how scarce parking is in our cities, especially in the large ones: a parking space in downtown New York can cost up to a million dollars. Not to mention all the pollution produced by driving around looking for parking, a substantial chunk of that 4% usage time. In short, traditional cars waste huge amounts of resources and pollute more than they should, with major negative impacts on the environment.

In my opinion, the self-driving car is the epitome of the transition to a digital economy, because once the (admittedly very complex) problem of car automation is solved, every other problem of collaborative robotics will easily be overcome.

A self-driving car absolutely requires all the technologies of the Fourth Industrial Revolution: Internet of Things, Big Data, Artificial Intelligence and advanced robotics. It is much more than a smartphone on four wheels, and its operation relies on a huge number of code lines.

	Machine	Year	Code lines	Notes
	Apollo 11	1969	140.000	Today an App has about 100,000 code lines
	Shuttle	2010	400.000	Control and guidance code only
	Boeing 787	2010	7.000.000	Avionics and online support systems
	Smartphone	2018	12.000.000	Android operating system
	Car	2020	100.000.000	L2/L3 high end cars

Table 3.2 Code lines required for the operation of some machines[88]

---

[88] https://www.informationisbeautiful.net/visualizations/million-lines-of-code/

Presently, a mid-to-high-end car already requires more than 100 million code lines, more than any other object in the world. And it is no wonder; after all, a car is the most sophisticated object you can build: it moves on almost any type of terrain and in any weather condition, and safety requirements are increasingly high, both relative to passengers and to external surroundings.

A car has to respond in real time even while running at very high speeds, and in very diverse situations.

It's a very complex environment to manage, but the moment we succeed, the doors of robotics will open wide. The advent of the self-driving car will start an extraordinary revolution in all areas.

3.6 From product to service: how price per kilo changes

The autonomous car example clearly shows the difference between the new pay-per-use model and the old ownership model. Knowing that a car, in Europe, weighs in average 1.4 tons and costs in average 27,500 euro and that it is used only 4% of the time, the cost-effectiveness, of using it instead of owning it, is self-evident.

Despite the fact that the car, from a software point of view, is becoming the most complex object there is, it is still inexpensive if we consider its price per kilo, which on average is around €20.

Prices range from €8 per kilo for a small city car to over €100 per kilo for a luxury sports car. Compared to a smartphone, an object that we all have in our pocket and that costs on average €2,000 per kilo, a car is really cheap.

But why is it that a car, which has so many electronics and so much code, is so much cheaper in terms of price per kilo than a smartphone? Because in a car there is a lot more matter: a smartphone weighs less than 200 grams whereas a car weighs over 1 ton.

Since the car's weight can hardly be reduced, we have to reduce the waste hidden in the 96% of time when it is not used. It is easy to see that customers would be better off buying the car's use.

What is more difficult to realize, but extremely interesting, is that manufacturers would also be better off selling the car's use, because they could then increase the price per kilo.

I would like to give an example (an oversimplified and somewhat crude example, as if a cow were spherical, just to get an intuitive idea) of how the service economy can dramatically increase the price per kilo of products used to provide the service.

Let's suppose we have a car that costs €20,000 and weighs 1 ton. Let's also suppose that the car has a service life of only 5 years and that at the end of this period the residual value is zero.

Now, based on this data, we can try to calculate the price per kilo of the car sold as a product and of the same car shared among a number of users.

Selling the car as a product: we divide the sale price of the car by the weight in kilos, i.e. €20,000/1000Kg = €20/Kg.

Selling the car as a service: we must first calculate how much a customer is willing to pay for the car's use. In our example we assume that he is willing to pay in five years the same amount that he would have paid to buy the car, and that the residual value of the car after five years is zero. This means that the customer will be willing to pay €20,000 over 5 years, that is €4,000 per year, for the car's use.

Now we need to calculate how many customers an autonomous car can serve. From statistical data we know that on average a car owner uses a car for 4% of the time of ownership.

Assuming for the sake of simplicity that the efficiency of use is 100%, we can conclude that a car can serve 25 subscribers to the service. We now have all the data to calculate the car's price per kilo in a pay-per-use scenario:

- Usage fee for each subscriber: €4,000/year
- Subscribers served by one car: 25
- Service life of the car: 5 years

By the fifth year, the service provider will have earned: €4,000/year*25 customers*5 years = €500,000. Assuming that the car weighs 1000Kg, this means having sold the car at a price of €500/Kg.

The price per kilo is 25 times greater! Within the same framework we could change all the parameters, for example we could assume that the customer wants to pay only €2,000 per year for the car's use and that the efficiency is only 50%, but we would still get a substantial price per kilo of €125.

This is the magic of digitization, which transforms inefficiencies into value for everyone: companies, customers and the environment. That's why car manufacturers are investing so much in the level 5 car.

With the huge amount of electronics and sensors that will be installed on board (lidar, radar, sonar, cameras), cars will become big data producers, and it is very likely that car manufacturers will gradually transform into software companies with large data centers.

To get an idea of the amount of data we are talking about here, consider that one single autonomous car will generate as much data as about 3,000 Internet users. This will inevitably change the way we look at cars.

Manufacturers will have to rethink their business models as well as their factories, and production sites will change beyond recognition: let's get ready for the emergence of data-driven car companies.

3.7 Overcoming resistance to the outcome economy

We cannot ignore the fact that the transition from the product economy to the service economy poses some risks and difficulties, but, as someone once said, "in the middle of difficulty lies opportunity"[89]. So, let's address these two aspects and see how difficulties can be overcome and risks mitigated.

The service economy is systemic; as such, it requires the active and synchronous participation of several actors, who must abandon their compartmentalized thinking and learn to operate according to an entirely new logic.

First of all, I believe that resistance to adopt the new business model of servitization is more cultural than financial, at least as far as design and production are concerned.

The design and production costs of a servitized product are in truth higher than those of a non-servitized product, but not so high as to cause a company's financial imbalance. However, what changes substantially is the capital required to activate and fuel the new business model.

While the traditional model allows a company to even out all the costs and raise a profit margin at the moment of sale, in the new model the company gets remunerated by the utilization or performance of the product.

This means that, although utilization and performance generate a steady cash flow, the collected fees can only even

---

[89] Wheeler J.A., *The Outsider* in Newsweek, vol. 93, no. 11, Mar. 12, 1979

out costs over time. Only after the costs have been covered can the generation of profit margin begin.

Production costs must be covered, as well as finance charges: the use of bank credit is inevitable because profits are delayed.

However, once these costs are absorbed, the fees earned on an on-going basis will allow for a very significant growth of the profit margin, because over time the costs sustained to provide the service grow much slower than the number of servitized products.

As we have seen in par. 3.4, in a digital economy the marginal cost of services tends to get close to zero with the increase of the customer base.

Once material products are servitized, they acquire the same property: their marginal cost also approaches zero, provided they are designed to be long-lived and high-quality products that are simple to use and efficient in delivering results.

Therefore, the problem for companies that are planning to servitize their products is to find financial instruments that can advance future subscription fees related to the service or pay-as-you-go model, so that at least production costs can be covered. It is a matter of finding a way to finance the working capital, that is, the capital required to manufacture the servitized products.

Many ways exist to finance the working capital during the transition from selling the product to selling the service associated with the product. I would like to give you an example that I find very interesting and instructive, even if it is not applicable to all products but only to those that can be used in sharing.

On the occasion of the announcement of the roll-out of a new service similar to Uber, Tesla CEO Elon Musk declared that the owners of a Tesla car could expect to earn an extra revenue of up to $30,000 per year by lending their car to the Tesla network when they do not need it[90].

As owners use their car for less than 5% of the time of ownership, this can certainly be seen as a way to get one's working capital financed.

Once the system reaches a critical mass with a sufficient cash flow from recurrent revenues from services, the need to finance the working capital is significantly reduced and companies can go back to more conventional modes of financing (or self-financing) their production activities.

In short, the banking system has to structure itself in such a way as to facilitate this transition which, as we have repeatedly said, is essential for the economy to continue growing in a sustainable way. In the industrial production model, banks already finance companies in the interval between the purchase of raw materials and the collection of profits after sale. In the new model, banks will have to advance the working capital for a much longer time, that is, from the purchase of raw materials until the moment when the pay-per-use fees will have covered the production costs plus a portion of the contribution margin. Just as we said, digitization changes everything, financing included.

In this regard, new methods will have to be developed to measure the creditworthiness of a servitized product. Simplifying access to credit for companies that choose the path of servitization will also accelerate the spread of sustainable practices and help the economy become increasingly circular.

---

[90] https://www.bizjournals.com/sanjose/news/2019/04/23/tesla-robotaxis-owners-earn-money-musk-tsla.html

Sustainability requires responsibility: all parties are concerned and must do their part.

But financing the working capital is not the only obstacle to the outcome economy.

The second problem is mitigating the risks linked to the product itself. In the industrial production mode, these risks are reduced by the transfer of ownership to the purchaser, whereas in the service economy the ownership always remains with the manufacturer, who must guarantee the asset's operational efficiency and take on all the related risks.

In the economic theories built upon the industrial model, insurance as well as other services are considered secondary to activities aimed at satisfying basic needs and tangible needs in general. But this is no longer true today.

Regardless of servitization, services can no longer be considered as secondary consumption.

Growth rates in the service sector exceed GDP growth rates, contradicting the classical and neo-classical economic thesis that services are not primary goods.

Besides, given the current complexity of economic systems, insurance services have become a fundamental tool for their correct operation.

As regards servitization, it is essential to design and implement specific types of product insurance, covering the risks of the manufacturer related to the correct operation of the product and to its effective capacity to provide the required service.

The costs related to this insurance are both a production cost and an ongoing cost for the entire useful life of the servitized product. Maintenance costs will also have to be included in the list of production costs and service costs, because with servitization spare parts and maintenance will no longer be a source of revenues.

For a provider who collects outcome fees, insurance, spare parts, repairs and routine maintenance are costs; this explains why he needs his products to have perfect operational efficiency and a very long useful life. The better his products are, the more will he earn from their servitization.

This transformation of revenues into costs is of course another obstacle to servitization. It is not a zero-cost transition, but the benefits in terms of future revenues are so interesting that they should convince companies to servitize their products.

What is certain is that products must be designed and engineered to be long-lasting, sturdy and quick to fix, which reverses the usual approach of the classic industrial production model.

Servitization requires us to abandon the traditional division among economic sectors. There is no longer a vertical divide between agriculture, industry and services, but rather a progressive inter-penetration and integration of all three.

Servitization does not mean that industrial production is entering the service sector, but that service activities are permeating all sectors. The whole economy is evolving because digitization addresses the intangible component of human needs.

Vertical farming is an interesting example of how all sectors are interpenetrating. In vertical farms that use aeroponics, vegetables are grown indoors in a limited space on super-imposed levels.

The roots are floating in the air and continuously sprayed with the right amount of water and with the right nutrients. Solar light is replaced by LED lamps with modulated light frequency.

This type of cultivation allows an increase in production of up to 400 times per square meter, if we consider the multiplication factor given by 24/7 production multiplied by the number of super-imposed levels that can be built. In vertical farms everything is controlled by digital technologies in real time, without pesticides, without waste of clear water or soil, and powered by energies that will increasingly come from renewable sources.

The production process no longer depends on unpredictable weather trends but is controlled by man and by technology. Vegetables can be produced according to real demand independently of the seasons, and they can actually go from the farm to the table.

As we can see, vertical farming provides a miraculous result: the production of edible plants gets servitized thanks to the interpenetration of all three economic sectors, which come together to create a more sustainable world.

PART IV

Examples of digitization and servitization

When digital transformation is done right,
it's like a caterpillar turning into a butterfly,
but when done wrong, all you have is
a really fast caterpillar.

George Westerman

4.1 The mutation ahead

As we have seen in Part II, Industry 4.0 is expected to evolve over time in four stages. The first two should take place in the short term, while the latter phase will develop over the medium term.

Short term:
1 - increase of operational efficiency
2 - new products combined with a host of services

Medium term:
3 - outcome economy
4 - autonomous economy in pull mode

To illustrate this impending mutation, I will provide some practical examples of the different stages. A fundamental aspect to consider is that these four stages can be addressed in a sequential order over time: applying a proper digitization process ensures that changes are incremental and can avoid a traumatic disruption.

It is essential to address digital transformation by implementing an architecture that provides reliable support through the entire process, because if the initial transformation is done properly, this will save both time and money in the future.

The first stage takes place inside the traditional industrial production model and, to quote Malaska[91], only intensifies

---

[91] *Ibid.*, Malaska P., *A Conceptual Framework for the Autopoietic Transformation of Societies*

results. Increased operational efficiency is the first advantage garnered from digitization.

For this reason, my advice to companies that are delaying the revision of their business model is to digitize their products, plants and machinery nonetheless. In this way, they can take advantage of an increased operational efficiency in the short term and be ready for the digital transformation when the time comes.

By correctly initiating the digitization process, with digital twins available both in real time and as historical sequences, companies will be able to shift from the product economy to the outcome economy quickly and painlessly.

Meanwhile, they can fully reap the benefits of an increased production efficiency, including improved maintenance services, predictive maintenance and higher customer satisfaction, to name a few.

The examples presented below are in no way exhaustive, and it will be easy for the reader to extrapolate other applications for different sectors.

4.2 The connected locomotive: an increase in operational efficiency

Let's start with a brown-field case in the rail freight sector: the digitization of a fleet of freight trains to improve operational efficiency and reduce locomotive downtime for maintenance operations.

Please recall the distinction between brown-field and green-field devices explained in Part II: existing non-connected objects - the vast majority on the market today - are grouped in the brown-field category; new-generation products, either connected or ready to be connected, belong to the green-field category.

To digitize a brown-field locomotive, we must first retrofit it with an IoT gateway. The IoT gateway will read the locomotive's sensors and send this data in real time, via a 3G/4G/5G network, to the IoT platform, which will collect it in a database (the data lake) and make it available to various applications.

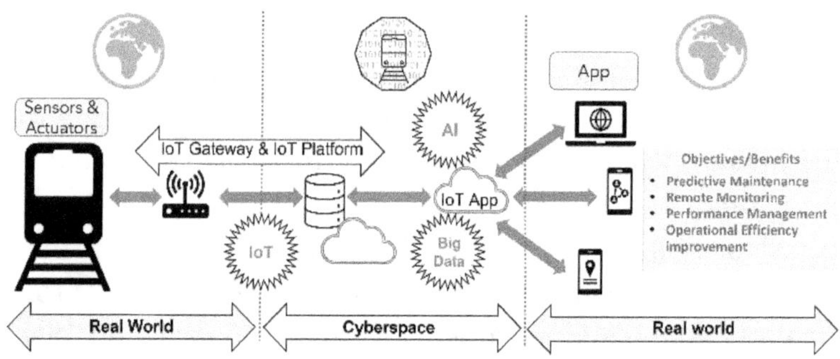

Figure 4.1 Digitization of a locomotive

The retrofit is a relatively easy operation, because currently train locomotives are equipped with an internal communication channel (bus) that carries both the data coming from the sensors and the data to be sent to the actuators. Basically, it is a matter of connecting an IoT gateway to the bus in read-only mode (so as not to interfere with the actuators), and of collecting (reading and storing) data from all the sensors at an established sampling rate. The IoT gateway will then organize the collected data into digital twins and send it to the IoT platform in the Cloud.

For this type of application, the customer might prefer, for data privacy reasons, to have the IoT platform installed on a private Cloud. The incoming data will either be stored in the data lake for future requests or sent in real time to the applications that have subscribed to the data receiving service.

Having access to historical and real-time data can be extremely cost-effective in any industry. According to some studies, it is possible to save up to 12% on scheduled repairs and to reduce maintenance costs by 30%, with the advantage of 70% fewer breakdowns[92].

Besides, with the digitization of machines, operators are no longer required to manually fill out forms and tables at the end of their shift, thus avoiding errors in compilation or interpretation. For locomotives we can imagine two main applications: implementation of predictive maintenance and optimization of logistics operations.

In the first use case, the existence of a digital twin changes maintenance from preventive to predictive: AI will help analyze the huge amount of data collected by the sensors on the train, in order to identify the parts at risk of impending failure and carry out maintenance in advance.

Real-time data from one locomotive allows short-term prediction of possible failures, while the analysis of historical data from the whole fleet allows failure prediction in the medium and long term. Therefore, instead of performing maintenance at regularly scheduled intervals as per normal routine, it will be possible to intervene only when necessary and, critically, before the failure occurs.

To make this possible, however, the accuracy of digital twins must be very high, with enough sensors to monitor all critical parts of the locomotive.

The certainty of knowing which parts are at risk of imminent failure means a fleet availability close to 100%, because the repairs of malfunctioning parts can be done when the locomotives are not in service: in the absence of a

---

[92] Sullivan G.P. et al., *Operations & Maintenance Best Practices: A Guide to Achieving Operational Efficiency*, Release 3.0, Pacific Northwest National Laboratory, U.S. Department of Energy. Aug. 2010

predictive maintenance strategy, roughly 10% of the fleet must remain on standby, ready to replace locomotives subject to sudden failure.

In conclusion, digitization allows a reduction of the operating costs for maintenance and for spare part inventories, against an increase in revenues due to a 100% operational availability and to the superior quality of the transport service offered.

In the second use case we can optimize logistics, thanks to the real-time knowledge of the location and status of all locomotives.

By combining this data with other information, for instance the coupling and uncoupling of wagons and the movements of goods, it is possible to plan transport activities with much greater efficiency.

Once the locomotive is equipped with a real-time connection to the Cloud, an electronic identification system could be designed for the carriages. By assigning a specific code to each wagon, we could monitor the entire train.

The availability in real time of the train's position, speed and acceleration, along with other data such as the condition of the brakes, would make it possible to avoid or reduce train accidents[93], providing yet another important benefit.

As we can see, a digitized locomotive becomes a service and is no longer a mere product. It is conceivable that, with the advent of digitization, train manufacturers will begin to think about changing their business model. In the short term, if locomotives are digitized at the factory (green-field scenario), manufacturers will be the first to have access to the vast amount of data produced; predictive maintenance itself will become a true service (predictive maintenance as-a-

---

[93] https://en.wikipedia.org/wiki/List_of_rail_accidents_(2020%E2%80%93present)

service) and be provided, along with other services, to freight companies.

When data begins to be monetized in these ways, transforming the business model will be a natural consequence in the medium term. This dynamic shows how data becomes more and more valuable over time, which leads to an increase in the price per kilo.

As soon as manufacturers realize that digitization can increase the price per kilo with a change of business model, they will be motivated to go from selling the locomotive as a product to selling its use or performance.

When products are connected and there are humans involved, we could apply the innovative and very interesting strategy of gamification. "Gamification is the strategic attempt to enhance systems, services, organizations, and activities to create similar experiences to those experienced when playing games, in order to motivate and engage users.

This is generally accomplished through the application of game-design elements and game principles (dynamics and mechanics) in non-game contexts"[94]. Gamification is very effective in aligning otherwise divergent interests and can be applied to any situation where humans and machines work in cooperation.

In the locomotive example, the players are the train drivers, and the game is to minimize the fuel/energy consumption through skilled and diligent driving; the most virtuous driver could be rewarded with a monthly prize.

Thanks to the digital twins present on all locomotives, every driver would be able to compare his own performance in real time with the performances of all the other drivers, and this would boost motivation and engagement.

---

[94] https://en.wikipedia.org/wiki/Gamification

This is just one simplified example; many other 'virtuous games' could be implemented across all fields.

4.3 The boiler of the future: a new product with new services

Let's now look at a case involving increased operational efficiency achieved not only through digitization, as in the case of the locomotive, but also through the development of a range of services associated with the product.

Let's take for example a gas boiler that is already in production or already installed, but not connected, basically a classic boiler used in home heating systems. Here, the problem is finding the right way to collect the boiler's operating data and send it to an IoT platform in the Cloud.

In almost all cases, the boiler is connected to a thermostat which sends it a single command: switch on and switch off. The thermostat either does not communicate with the user, or gives the user very little information, such as the current temperature of the room and the on/off status of the boiler. Newer boilers, on the other hand, have an internal communication channel (bus) which allows a bidirectional exchange of information between the boiler and the thermostat.

This data is used to regulate a number of parameters for the resident's comfort and for improved diagnostics, but it is only available locally, that is, if the user or the technician are physically present on site.

If the thermostat only sends the boiler the command to switch on and off, we are still in the brown-field category, therefore a retrofit is necessary: an IoT gateway must be installed, which communicates both with the boiler itself and with the IoT platform in the Cloud.

This is a much simpler operation than in the case of the locomotive, given the much smaller number of sensors and actuators that have to be read and controlled. Moreover, the frequency of data update required for a boiler is lower compared to a locomotive, because the heating dynamics of a boiler are much slower than the movement dynamics of a locomotive that can travel at more than 100 Km per hour.

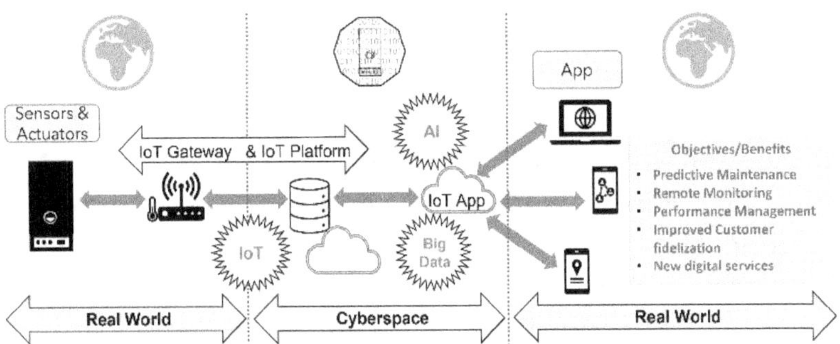

Figure 4.2 Digitization of a boiler

The retrofit operation will almost always be performed at the factory because it is easy to turn a traditional boiler into a connected one; the required changes are minimal and there is no need to redesign the boiler, provided however that the IoT gateway is able to 'talk' to the boiler's control unit (the embedded computer).

If the boiler is already equipped with a bus and communicates with the thermostat, the most convenient solution for the manufacturer is to redesign the thermostat by adding the IoT gateway function. In this case the boiler belongs to the green-field category.

Following the retrofit or redesign, the boiler's thermostat will now have, in addition to the traditional function of controlling operations and programming the desired temperature, the function of sending the collected data to the IoT platform. In this use case data is not very critical, therefore the IoT platform can be installed on a public Cloud.

As in the case of the locomotive, the IoT platform receives the data, then either stores it or sends it to the applications. Here too, we can imagine several scenarios. Let's see some of them.

The first scenario is an app for manufacturers. The app sends manufacturers real time data from the connected boilers, allowing them to know exactly when and where they have been installed.

Thanks to this data, manufacturers will be able to compile important case histories regarding the use and operation of their boilers, and to quickly make improvements as needed.

Manufacturers will also use the collected data for marketing purposes, because these data will be enriched over time by customers using their own app.

The second scenario concerns the maintenance network. Each technician will have access to real-time data regarding the status of the boilers under his responsibility and will receive real-time alerts about any anomalies or breakdowns.

This will allow him to optimize his repair and maintenance operations, saving time and money: as we have seen, the payoff obtained through improved maintenance activities is considerable.

The availability of historical data from the entire fleet would make it possible to establish statistical models for boiler failures and thus transform repairs.

Currently, repair costs are calculated based on a technician's time and on the spare parts used; in our example, they would be converted to an annual subscription fee, in the same way as any insurance.

The third scenario is an app for the end customer, and it can be used in several ways.

First, it works with a smart thermostat and gives the user the possibility to remotely program the boiler, as a way to reduce consumption and increase comfort.

Second, the app provides a privileged communication channel with the maintenance service, so as to simplify any technical interventions.

Third, the same app allows the manufacturer to stay in touch with his customers, meaning he can both profile them more accurately and have an opportunity for up-selling, that is, proposing further products or services based on the use of the boiler and on the temperatures measured during the year.

For example, it could be inferred from data collected during the summer season that some customers do not own an air conditioner.

Based on this data, the manufacturer could launch a promotional campaign for the sale of air conditioners, possibly through the same app. In this scenario, customer loyalty is increased by frequent contact and the company brand gets stronger.

In these examples of digitization, it is easy to see that what matters is not so much the product itself as the way it is used and the performance it can deliver. In the two cases of the locomotive and the boiler, which can be extended to many other sectors and situations, we are still at the first stage, where a product, existing or new, is optimized in terms of efficiency and enriched with services.

The next step is to change the business model altogether, completing the transition from the sale of products to the sale of services. Although we are currently still at the starting line, we must remember that "everything cyberizable will be in cyberspace"[95] and that all products will be digitized and become services in the end.

4.4 Towards the outcome economy: industrial machines

Let's now look at the transformation from product to service in the industrial sector. The industrial machinery manufacturing sector is still almost entirely based on the sale of equipment, often combined with the sale of maintenance services. Here are some examples of sectors that might benefit from a change of business model.

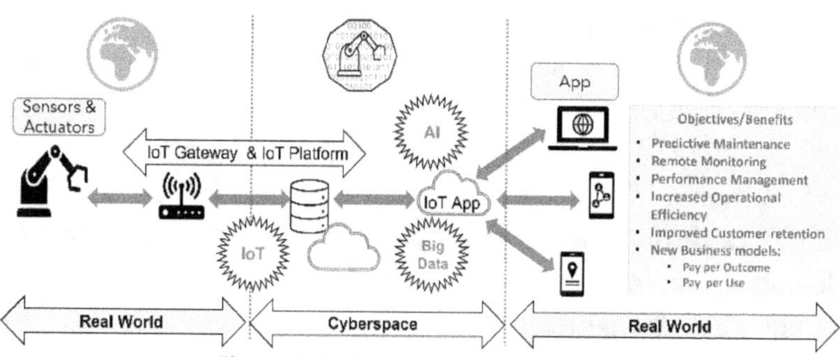

Figure 4.3 Digitization of machinery

Let's start with the case of a manufacturer of industrial inkjet printers. In the traditional industrial sales model, the connection of the printer to the Cloud in IoT mode is seen as an extra cost that cannot be passed on to the customer.

By selling unconnected printers, however, the manufacturer is unable to control the type and quantity of inks used, and therefore fails to offer his customers recommendations for timely replacements of ink cartridges, which could provide an attractive recurring revenue stream.

---

[95] Bell G., Gray J., ACM's 50th Anniversary Conference, San Jose, CA 1997

In addition, the customer's use of inks with a chemical composition different than expected could lead to higher-than-budgeted maintenance and/or repair costs, on which maintenance contracts have been calculated.

These problems can be solved by producing printers connected in IoT mode, that is, connected to an IoT gateway that sends their digital twins to the IoT platform in the Cloud.

With connected printers, things improve significantly for the manufacturer, and customer satisfaction grows as well. Thanks to data collected in real time by the IoT platform and to the applications that rely on this data, the manufacturer can monitor on an ongoing basis the ink consumption levels, the number of refills made and the quality of the inks used.

Furthermore, data collected from the sensors will provide even more information: the condition of the inkjet head, the operating temperature, the electrical connection, the voltage and so on. With all this data, it becomes easy to draw a detailed plan for ink supplies and maintenance. It is also possible to change the sales policy, for example implementing a pay-as-you-go model that only requires an initial fee for the printer's installation, counting on revenues deriving from the sale of inks and from the use of the printer.

Let's now turn our attention to another type of industrial machines, that perform precise and measurable repetitive actions or that produce parts. If we take for instance a bottling machine, we can realistically assume that the buyer wants to buy the bottling function, not the machine itself.

By equipping the machine with the right sensors, it becomes possible to charge customers for the machine's operation (that is, the number of bottles actually filled) rather than for the machine itself. The same sales model could be applied to other industrial equipment, such as aluminum die-casting machines, looms, and any other complex machine for materials production and processing.

Many expensive machines have qualities that are not immediately visible, such as durability, total cost of maintenance, time between breakdowns, out-of-service time and estimated useful life. These qualities are notoriously difficult to sell, especially when similar machines, coming from countries where labor costs are minimal, are available at a much lower price. Typically, the customer tends to focus on the purchase price.

In most cases, specifying that the machine is more expensive because it is built to last longer is not a convincing argument: in the current industrial production model, short-term savings are almost always the determining factor. Yet, it is precisely this model that is making our economy unsustainable.

Conversely, the service economy model offers a different solution and the benefits are twofold: on one hand, the new model allows the supervising manager to achieve his short-term objectives (buying at the lowest price), and on the other hand it allows the company to achieve its long-term objectives (affordable cost of machine management).

Finally, it also helps the company meet its ESG (Environmental, Social & Governance) objectives, since the purchase of the service instead of the machinery supports the circular economy.

Once the machine is digitized, selling the service makes the producer more competitive because he can now sell the use of the machine based on a subscription model with a fixed and/or variable fee, thus saving his customers a significant initial investment.

In other words, customers can turn Capex (**Cap**ital **ex**penditure: buying the machine) into Opex (**Op**erating

expenditure: buying the use of the machine according to production needs). At the same time, the manufacturer is not forced to lessen his machines' quality or to relocate production in order to keep low prices.

Each manufacturer will find ways to differentiate fees based on the number of pieces produced, on energy consumption or on other performances, depending on each sector of activity. In the case of a loom, for example, customers could be charged based on the length of the woven fabrics, on the intricacy of the patterns or on the wear and tear of the machine during operation.

Of course, these are only basic ideas on the subject; clearly manufacturers can think of other and more suitable models for monetizing machine performance.

To measure with numbers the positive effects of servitization on sales, it is interesting to do an analysis of revenue trends over the past five years for companies in the manufacturing sector. In 2020, this sector was affected by supply issues and budget cuts due to the COVID-19 pandemic. Compared to the last quarter of 2019, sales of manufacturing companies in the S&P 500 fell by nearly 14%. However, if we look at companies offering advanced services through subscriptions, we can see that since the last quarter of 2019, their revenues have instead increased by nearly 6%[96]. If we analyze the sales trend, from the beginning of 2018 until the start of the pandemic, these same companies experienced a 50% growth in revenues, compared to a 10% decline for the others.

If we look at the sales performance of these two classes of companies from the beginning of 2018 to the end of 2022,

---

[96] The Subscription Economy Index, Subscribed Institute, March 2023, https://www. subscribedinstitute.com

the companies in the S&P500 index experienced growth with a CAGR of just over 4%, while the servitized companies experienced growth with a CAGR of over 16%.

These data can only confirm the importance of digital transformation and product servitization.

4.5 From connected machines to connected factories

Now let's look at factory management, and let's see how it will evolve in the new outcome economy. Once all machines are connected, data management inside the factory will change from a hierarchical model based on a SCADA (Supervisory Control And Data Acquisition) architecture to a model that I like to call 'federated' around a data lake.

I will describe this new model with the help of the diagram presented below.

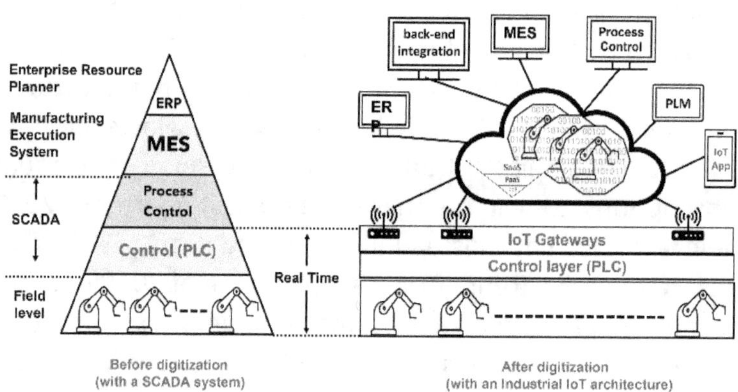

Figure 4.4 SCADA and Industrial IoT: from a hierarchical to a federated data structure

In the traditional factory model, the backbone consists of a SCADA architecture which handles the acquisition and control of data coming from all the machinery.

This is a very rigid hierarchical structure where software applications are one inside the other and data is trapped in the data silos of each single application, making its subsequent retrieval very difficult.

Although the SCADA architecture represented a big step ahead when it was first implemented, it certainly lacks flexibility: changing the functions of the system or adding new functions is extremely complex and burdensome because we are forced to work backwards and modify the entire hierarchical data chain in reverse.

The new Industrial IoT architecture, on the contrary, is no longer arranged in a hierarchical manner, but rather according to a 'federated' model around the data lake powered by the IoT itself. That is to say, all software applications are on the same level and any one of them can directly access any data.

The result is an extremely agile structure that makes it possible to easily upgrade, modify, adapt or expand the machines' functions, as well as to apply technological innovations that improve the plant's efficiency over time.

The difference between the two models is not insignificant: although at first glance the data representation looks the same, the two cases are by no means equivalent. Unfortunately, due to their apparent similarity SCADA solutions are often passed off for Industrial IoT.

But we must not forget that, even though both models are data driven, the first one makes data difficult to access and almost useless for new implementations and for deriving future insights, while the second model makes data easily available and manageable, with huge benefits for factory management.

4.6 Wide-ranging effects of the outcome economy

Servitization and the outcome economy will bring about many changes in our way of life and in society as a whole. While it is difficult for us today to clearly anticipate all these changes, examining the repercussions of the emergence of the self-driving car on a broader and more general level offers a taste of what is to come.

First of all, having a self-driving car at one's disposal will dissuade people from buying cars; in fact, they will increasingly rely on car service providers. In my opinion, this is the main reason why major car manufacturers are making big investments to achieve level 5 autonomy: they have understood that they can earn much more from selling the car's use than from selling the car.

That said, many other sectors could be reoriented starting with insurance companies, due to the drastic reduction in road accidents. According to WHO sources[97], road traffic crash deaths are currently around 1.3 million a year, and it is estimated that autonomous cars will save more than one million lives a year. In view of this change, some insurance companies are already offering policies based on the use and not on the ownership of vehicles.

Regardless, the downsizing of car insurance policies will be amply compensated, because the shift from product to service will compel manufacturers to ensure all their products. The dramatic decrease in accidents and injuries will also reduce civil lawsuits and criminal trials with a decrease in jobs for specialized attorneys.

The repair industry will be very much impacted by self-driving cars, because damage to car bodies will become sporadic and mechanical breakdowns increasingly unlikely.

---

[97] https://www.who.int/news-room/fact-sheets/detail/road-traffic-injuries

As I have repeatedly pointed out, when we sell the product's use we need the product to perform perfectly for a very long time, and this means it will be designed in a completely different way. In addition, thanks to the large amount of data collected and sent by the car, predictive maintenance will be applied and impending failures will be identified in advance.

Trucking services and cabs will undergo a major downsizing, as drivers will no longer be needed. In the car rental sector, companies will start renting out autonomous cars not for whole days but only for the time of use, and car rental services that include a driver will disappear.

Great news for a company like Uber: I think this is exactly what it has been waiting for to finally see its business model take off.

More generally, the proliferation of self-driving cars will change people's lifestyle habits. Air travel on short routes will most likely be avoided for reasons of convenience, productivity, and in many cases, time saving. Stops at roadside rest areas will also be drastically reduced: once on board, people will just enter the coordinates of their destination and then do something else; there will be no need for rest breaks due to weariness, that then translate into food and drink consumption at service stations.

Finally, the demand for fuel will decrease, not only because of the rising number of electric vehicles, but also because time will no longer be wasted in search of parking spaces, and clumsy or inexpert driving will disappear.

Needless to say, the demand for garages and parking lots in cities will also drop dramatically. Driving schools will largely disappear, because driving will be a hobby and no longer a necessary skill. Autonomous cars will also have a big impact on elderly care and childcare, where driving assistance is essential.

A model of connected public transport will undoubtedly improve transport services in a given territory, because it will reach on demand, and only when necessary, areas with low population density where a bus service with driver is today economically unviable.

If we add self-driving cars offering quick, direct and easy-to-book journeys, it is easy to infer a rise in demand for housing in inland and suburban areas, now unattractive - not for lack of scenery or of quality of life - but for lack of services that could solve the problem of distance from work, schools and recreational activities.

Consequently, the value of residential property in peripheral locations will also rise, because people will no longer need to live in the city center.

Remote working will be available to anyone, wherever they live, provided they have access to a broadband digital connection. The so-called digital divide will decide whether someone has the opportunity of working from home or not and will therefore make a growing difference in terms of the attractiveness of a place. And it is easy to see the huge advantage that could come from the combination of smart working with on-demand self-driving cars as an alternative to public transport.

A person living in a quaint little village could work from the comfort of their home; should they need to commute into the city or out of the region for work or personal reasons, they could sit comfortably in a self-driving car and, while the car manages everything, use the commute time to work, read, exercise, relax, eat or sleep.

As for businesses like restaurants and stores, they will be able to provide vastly improved home delivery services, both more efficient and cheaper, thereby increasing their customer base.

Car design will certainly change dramatically: the interior will look more like an office or a living room. Some even anticipate that cars will turn into travelling gyms and that commute time will be used for sports. Finally, since each self-driving car will produce Terabytes of data daily, car manufacturers will focus much more on data management than on industrial production.

Apart from the big changes brought about by the self-driving car, the digital economy will impact many other aspects of our social and economic life.

For instance, small businesses will become competitive again and will coexist with large e-commerce platforms, firstly because they will be able to provide traditional products and services for their local community, and secondly because they will focus on the "long tail"[98], that is, selling low volumes of hard-to-find items to many widespread customers. As the long tail is always scattered geographically, the Internet will play an essential role in helping small businesses find a global market niche for their products.

Digitization techniques designed for smart cities will be applied to inland areas with low population density, which by analogy are called 'smart lands'[99].

While in smart cities data collection is mainly used for traffic control, crowd management, security, energy saving and urban decorum, in smart lands it could also be used to provide digital services in replacement of local services that are no longer economically viable.

---

[98] Anderson C., *The Long Tail: Why the Future of Business Is Selling Less of More*, Hyperion Books, New York 2006
[99] Bonomi A., Masiero R., *Dalla smart city alla smart land*, Marsilio, Venezia 2014

With digitization, a community scattered across a vast territory can become a unified and cohesive community in the digital realm, thanks to the virtual aggregation of people. In secluded locations where the disappearance of many services represents a major challenge, the implementation of suitable IoT architectures can provide interesting economies of scale.

With pervasive broadband, connected homes, sensorized roads and squares, and an adequate digital literacy, local brick-and-mortar businesses could be replaced by much more efficient digital services such as telemedicine, online pharmacy, distance education, e-commerce and mobile offices operating year-round, 24/seven.

The digital transformation of the economy could invert or at least mitigate the projected trend toward urbanization, according to which 68% of the world population will be living in urban areas by 2050[100]. The new digital production model does not require, like the industrial model, a separation between the city, the periphery and the countryside.

The world population could be redistributed more evenly, because digital technology can bring back to life all the areas forgotten by the industrial economy. It has the power to bring the periphery back to the center. Marginality will no longer be a matter of geographical location, but a matter of digital connection.

More importantly, the digital transformation will free up time and give it back to people and to self-care: in this sense, we can certainly say that technology will improve the quality of our lives. The digital world is already at our doorstep; although it may still seem far away, it will soon become our everyday reality.

---

[100] https://www.un.org/sustainabledevelopment/blog/2018/05/68-of-the-world-population-projected-to-live-in-urban-areas-by-2050-says-un/

All technologies create better connections between humans, and digital technologies are the most powerful and functional for this purpose: the IoT, digital twins, telecommunication networks, 5G, Artificial Intelligence and collaborative robots like autonomous vehicles will ferry us to Society 5.0, the super smart society of the future.

4.7 The future production system: from push to pull

Once the new business models of the outcome economy have been widely adopted, the last stage of the digital transformation will begin. This last stage will gradually lead to the complete autonomy of the manufacturing process.

The widespread use of smart objects and cobots will radically transform the working environment, because it will change the way production is planned. There will be a gradual shift from push to pull, that is, from a supply driven to a demand driven production mode.

By analyzing the logics of push and pull production, we will understand why digitization is necessarily at the root of this evolution.

The push mode has been at the base of mass production for the entire duration of the twentieth century and is still largely predominant in the industry today. This mode is driven by supply, that is, based on the production of goods that are most likely to be sold.

Basically, companies estimate customer demand in advance, then manufacture standard products and finally 'push' these products onto the market using their own distribution channels and through marketing campaigns.

The pull mode is demand-driven, and therefore much more open and flexible. In pull mode customers, so to speak, 'pull' the products they want from manufacturers.

This mode relies on platforms that aggregate a large number of goods suppliers and that dynamically manage a wide range of resources and materials needed for production.

Companies that apply a digital manufacturing model assemble increasingly customized products that meet local or specific requirements. Since they use very fast manufacturing processes, they are able to quickly respond to customers' needs.

To detect demand in real time, production systems must be connected in a network where each node is highly automated and specialized, and at the same time very flexible in order to adapt to rapidly changing demand.

In the new digital economy, companies are aware that trying to anticipate demand is pointless and that in a digital marketplace customers have much more power than in the past.

The Fordist mass production model, where a customer "can have a car painted any color he wants as long as it's black",[101] is over. Soon, everyone will have exactly the car they want with the color they prefer, and they will have it for that specific trip. And for their next trip? Another model, another color, because this is the age of mass customization.

Demand niches, that is, the long tails of the demand curve, are impossible to satisfy in push mode, but they become a very interesting market segment if addressed in pull mode. This is why businesses are rapidly growing in this new segment, which has long been ignored by traditional production.

The pull phenomenon, born within the digital world, is now contaminating all sectors as they become digitized and

---

[101] Ford H., Crowther S., *My Life and Work*, Doubleday, Page & Company 1922

they begin to build their business models around data and intangible assets.

The digital production model does not discriminate between a service offering a piece of music and a service delivered by a gas boiler. Once digitized, every activity takes on the same appearance, and shifting from push to pull comes naturally because being digital means above all communicating, and therefore listening.

By its very nature, the pull logic is much more powerful in attracting customers, because it allows co-creation and, by extending the concept of prosumer, also co-production.

A huge transformation is already under way: it will impact all production activities and will be inclusive to all domains: social life, art, education, politics, government etc.

In the words of Roberto Masiero[102], when the production mode changes, everything, and I mean every single thing, changes.

---

[102] *Ibid.* Masiero R., *La società circolare*

Conclusion

*Digital is the main reason just over half of the companies
on the Fortune 500 have disappeared since the year 2000.*
Pierre Nanterme

*There is no alternative to digital transformation.
Visionary companies will carve out new
strategic options for themselves
- those that don't adapt, will fail.*
Jeff Bezos

We have learned from the past and we are learning from the present that the industrial production mode, by the very nature of its design, can harm and disrupt human society. Despite its significant contribution to humanity's progress, and the reduction of poverty we have witnessed over the course of the last century, we must now acknowledge that the demands of our growing population can't be met by such an unsustainable economic model.

Industrial production as currently practiced can lead to different future scenarios, some of them probable, others only possible. If we continue to do what we have always done, this will probably lead to economic and social collapse according to the World3 simulation.

Not all scenarios forecast the worst, but if we maintain the industrial production mode, all the technological advances and changes in human behavior will not prevent our decline: the outcome will be at best a stabilized world without further growth. Like Giarini[103], I believe that this limit is intrinsic to the industrial production system, and that the only solution is to change the production model and to undertake the transition from the ownership of products to the use of products, thereby putting in place a circular economy[104].

In this context, new digital technologies are crucial, because they enable the shift from industrial production (satisfying tangible needs) to digital production (satisfying intangible needs).

Thanks to the pervasiveness of computers and communications, it is possible to collect data from connected products in real time and to transform it into information.

As we know, uncertainty about the future behavior of products and about the performance of servitized products represents the greatest obstacle to the adoption of the outcome economy; the information generated by connected products will progressively eliminate this uncertainty and guarantee a high level of predictability.

In fact, information will help us reduce and mitigate uncertainty to the point that the digital production system will become viable and economically appealing for all industries.

The digital production system offers another major advantage compared to the industrial system, in that it resolves the conflict between the goals of the economy and the ambitions of human society.

Economic actors look for short term profits, in contrast with the main pursuit of human society, which should be to

---

[103] Giarini O., *New Paradigm in the Service Economy - The Search of Economics for Scientific Credibility: In between Hard and Soft Sciences* – in Cadmus vol. 2, no. 3, 2014

[104] Stahel W.R., *The Circular Economy, a User's Guide*, Routledge, Oxon and New York 2019

increase the well-being of future generations. Digital production and servitization can align the interests of all actors, allowing companies to enjoy long lasting profits while at the same time increasing human welfare and preserving the environment.

Digital production can help us build a more secure future, according to the World3 best-case scenario. By reorienting ourselves towards a servitized circular economy, we can substantially multiply the final value in terms of utilization rate and increased cost per kilo of goods, with the same tangible output.

It would be interesting to develop a totally new World3-type simulation tool based on the new emerging digital production model. World3 has had its day; it is time to move on to a different model that demonstrates the full potential of digital production and of product servitization. A new model would deepen our understanding of the future that awaits us, and I am certain that many of its scenarios would be sustainable.

To enable the changes I have described in this book, we need to invest extensively in education because the new production system is going to require new skills, just as new skills have been essential to the transition from the agricultural age to the industrial age. Indeed, as the objects that surround us and the production machines become smart, the human component, and above all human creativity, will become increasingly relevant, both in everyday life and within the work arena.

All manufacturing industries will use highly automated smart machinery which will lower production costs and raise the quality of products. At the same time, the complete automation of factories will free people from repetitive work, so that they can shift their focus to quintessential human activities, such as creative problem solving and collaboration.

In order to increase general productivity and at the same time benefit from a dynamic and engaging work experience, humans of the future will necessarily have to cooperate with machines.

The IoT, Big Data, Artificial Intelligence and robotics will steer the world towards a new production mode based on intangible assets, and the new workforce will include both humans and machines.

Due to the exponential growth of computing power, joining forces with machines will be inevitable, so much so that we can speak - in the words of Giuseppe O. Longo[105] - of a co-evolution between humans and machines.

This increasingly harmonious and symbiotic integration will generate results that neither men nor machines could ever achieve by themselves. In the meantime, we will experience the Metaverse: in this new arena, humans will interact with the digital twins of machines and, before long, digital twins of humans will interact with digital twins of machines. These interactions in the cyberspace will change both the virtual and the physical reality.

This 'human-centered automation', along with a new production mode increasingly based on the satisfaction of intangible needs, is likely to create many new jobs as well as redefine the way we work.

We live in a century of exponential technological progress that compels us to become life-long learners, a reality that is dramatically true for younger generations.

---

[105] Longo G.O., *L'avvento di Homo technologicus*, https://www.scienzainrete.it 2015

I reflect on this with great optimism knowing that as true digital natives, boys and girls of the future will be much better equipped to address and maneuver continuous change.

As Alvin Toffler said quoting psychologist Herbert Gerjuoy, "the new education must teach the individual (...) how to teach himself. Tomorrow's illiterate will not be the man who can't read, he will be the man who has not learned how to learn"[106].

The future workforce and society will undergo a radical change, and it would be no surprise if this led to full employment, as predicted by Orio Giarini[107].

Furthermore, the new mode of production and consumption will demonetize and democratize the access to the use of products, thus creating a better and more equitable world.

The quantum leap from the satisfaction of tangible needs to the satisfaction of intangible needs will require a pervasive use of automation, with intelligent machines leaving the more creative and relational components to humans. In fact, technologies are designed to empower rather than replace people, and they are essential precisely because they can put humans and their needs at the center.

Many hold the limited view that fully automated production represents a threat to human jobs, but only because they think new technologies and robotization will simply be applied to reinforce the traditional production mode. But this will not happen: the value of new technologies lies precisely in the fact that they allow a radical change of paradigm, the rise of a totally new production mode.

---

[106] *Ibid.*, Toffler A., *Future Shock*
[107] *Ibid.*, Giarini O., Liedtke P.M., *The Employment Dilemma and the Future of Work*

Everything is simply a consequence of the production mode in place: digital technologies facilitate our access to a new era of growth and prosperity, not by intensifying industrial production but by overcoming it.

Humans tend to imagine the future as a linear continuation of the past: the truth is that the future is exponential compared to the past, and that it will be completely and surprisingly different.

We live in a period that has no precedent in the history of mankind: technology is advancing at an astonishingly fast pace, so much so that in this century alone we will see the equivalent (at the current growth rate) of what has been accomplished by the human species in twenty thousand years[108].

The fact that we are increasingly interconnected means that human knowledge is expanding at a rate that was unimaginable only a decade ago. There have never been so many opportunities to create businesses that can change the world for the better.

The transition to the digital production mode is vital. We have the technologies, we have the economic models, and we have digital natives who are naturally oriented to the satisfaction of intangible need and open to sharing goods and buying their use or performance.

Now we need a new generation of entrepreneurs who strongly believe in the great possibilities of digitization: a young entrepreneurial class that understands and employs the powerful means only technology can offer to create a sustainable economy that will bring benefits and opportunities for everyone.

---

[108] *Ibid.*, Kurzweil R., *The Singularity is Near*

BIBLIOGRAPHY

Anderson C., *The Long Tail: Why the Future of Business Is Selling Less of More*, Hyperion Books, New York 2006

Bell G., Gray J., ACM's 50th Anniversary Conference, San Jose, CA 1997

Bolt J. and van Zanden J.L., *Maddison Project Database*, Maddison style estimates of the evolution of the world economy. A new 2020 update, https://www.rug.nl/ggdc/historicaldevelopment/maddison/releas es/maddison-project-database-2020?lang=en

Bonomi A., Masiero R., *Dalla smart city alla smart land*, Marsilio, Venezia 2014

Boulding K.E., *The Economics of the Coming Spaceship Earth*, in Environmental Quality Issues in a Growing Economy, 1966

Buckminster Fuller R., *Nine Chains to the Moon*, J.B. Lippincott Co, Philadelphia 1938

Calvino I., *Invisible Cities*, Harcourt Brace & Company, New York 1974

Clarke A.C., The three laws: https://en.wikipedia.org/wiki/Clarke's_three_laws

Data sources 1840-1900: R.E. Gallman and T.J. Weiss, *The Service Industries in the Nineteenth Century*, in Production and Productivity in the Service Industries, Victor Fuchs ed.

Data sources 1950-2010: Bureau of Economic Analysis, National Income and Product

Data sources 1900-1940: J.W. Kendrick, *Productivity Trends in the United States*, Princeton, Princeton University Press, 1961

De Toni A.F., Siagri R., Battistella C., *Corporate Foresight: Anticipating the Future*, Routledge, Oxon 2017

Diamandis P.H., Kotler S., *Abundance: The Future Is Better Than You Think*, Free Press, New York 2012

Drexler K.E., *Nanosystems: Molecular Machinery, Manufacturing, and Computation*, Wiley Interscience, New York 1992

Eliot T.S., *Burnt Norton* in *Four Quartets*, Faber and Faber, London 1940-42

Feynman R., Talk at the annual meeting of the American Physical Society, Dec. 1959; https://www.calteches.library.caltech.edu/47/2/1960Bottom.pdf

Ford H., Crowther S., *My Life and Work*, Doubleday, Page & Company 1922

Gershenfeld N., *When Things Start to Think*, Henry Holt & Company, New York 1999

Giarini O., Liedtke P.M., *The Employment Dilemma and the Future of Work*, Report to the Club of Rome, The Geneva Association 1996

Giarini O., *New Paradigm in the Service Economy - The Search of Economics for Scientific Credibility: In between Hard and Soft Sciences* – in Cadmus vol 2, no. 3, 2014

Giarini O., Stahel W.R., *The Limits to Certainty*, Kluwer Academic Publishers 1989

Guillemette Y., Turner D., *The Long View: Scenarios for the World Economy to 2060*, Economic Policy Paper no. 22, OECD Publishing 2018

Harich J., *Change Resistance as the Crux of the Environmental Sustainability Problem*, in System Dynamics Review, vol. 26, no.1, Jan.-Mar. 2010

Harper's New Monthly Magazine, vol. XII, no. LXVIII, Jan. 1856

Interim Report for the Decadal Plan for Semiconductors, SIA, SRC; https://www.semiconductors.org/wp-content/uploads/2020/10/Decadal-Plan_Interim-Report.pdf

Kurzweil R., *The Law of Accelerating Returns*, 2001: https://www.kurzweilai.net/the-law-of-accelerating-returns

Kurzweil R., *The Singularity is Near*, Viking Press, New York 2005

Landauer R., *Information is Physical*, Physics Today, American Institute of Physics, May 1961

Lloyd S., *Ultimate Physical Limits to Computation*, in Nature, vol. 406, no. 6788, Aug. 2000

Longo G.O., *Homo technologicus*, Meltemi, Roma 2001

Longo G.O., *Il simbionte. Prove di umanità futura*, Meltemi, Roma 2003

Longo G.O., *L'avvento di Homo technologicus*, https://www.scienzainrete.it 2015

Machiavelli N., *The Prince*, translated by W.K. Marriott, release date Mar. 1998; https://www.gutenberg.org/ebooks/1232

Malaska P., *A Conceptual Framework for the Autopoietic Transformation of Societies*, FUTU-publication 5/99, 1999; https://www.utu.fi/fi/yksikot/ffrc/tutkimus/hankearkisto/Documents/futu_5_99.pdf

Masiero R. et al., *La società circolare. Fordismo, capitalismo molecolare, sharing economy*, DeriveApprodi, Roma 2016

Masiero R., *Dopo la tecnica*, awaiting publication

McCarthy J., *Time-Sharing Computer Systems* in Management and the Computer of the Future, Martin Greenberger Ed., The MIT Press, Cambridge MA 1962

Meadows D. et al., *The Limits to Growth. A Report for the Club of Rome's Project on the Predicament of Mankind*, Potomac Associates, 1972

Meadows D., Meadows D., Randers J., *Beyond the Limits* (Hardcover ed.), Chelsea Green Publishing, 1992 ISBN 0-930031-55-5

Meadows D., Randers J., Meadows D., *Limits To Growth*: The 30-Year Update (Paperback ed.), Chelsea Green Publishing, June 2004 ISBN 193149858X

Miller G., *Informavores*, in The Study of Information, F. Machlup and U. Mansfield (eds),Wiley 1983

Negroponte N., *Being Digital*, A. Knopf, New York 1995

Nielsen, The Sustainability Imperative, New Insights on Consumer Expectations, Oct. 2015; https://www.nielsen.com/wp-content/uploads/sites/3/2019/04/Global20Sustainability20Report_October202015.pdf

Pasqualino R., Demartini M., Bagheri F., *Digital Transformation and Sustainable Oriented Innovation: A System Transition Model for Socio-Economic Scenario Analysis*, in Sustainability, 2021, 13, 11564

Peccei A., *The Human Quality*, Pergamon Press 1977

Pirolli P., *Information Foraging Theory: Adaptive Interaction with Information*, Oxford University Press, New York 2007

Reed D.P., *The Law of the Pack*, in Harvard Business Review, March 2001

Rees M., *On the Future: Prospects for Humanity*, Princeton University Press, 2018

Scher R., *Leveling the Playing Field*, Rowman & Littlefield, Guilford CT 2016

Schouw B., https://blog.softwareag.com/iot-digital-twins-metaverse

Schrödinger E., *What is Life? The Physical Aspect of the Living Cell*, University Press, Cambridge 1944

Schwab K., *The Fourth Industrial Revolution*, World Economic Forum 2016

Siagri R., *Pervasive Computers and the Grid: the Birth of a Computational Exoskeleton for Augmented Reality*, ACM Proceedings of ESEC-FSE'07: https://dl.acm.org/doi/abs/10.1145/1287624.1287626

Simon H.A., *The Architecture of Complexity*, Proceedings of the American Philosophical Society, vol. 106, no. 6, Dec. 1962

Smart J., Cascio J., Paffendorf J., https://www.metaverseroadmap.org/overview/

Smart J., https://www.accelerationwatch.com/laws.html#tech

Stahel W.R., *The Circular Economy - A User's Guide*, Routledge, Oxon and New York 2019

Stahel W.R., *The Performance Economy*, Palgrave Macmillan, London 2006

Stephenson N., *Snow Crash*, Bantam Books, New York 1992

Sullivan G.P. et al., *Operations & Maintenance Best Practices: A Guide to Achieving Operational Efficiency*, Release 3.0, Pacific Northwest National Laboratory, U.S. Department of Energy. Aug. 2010

Teilhard de Chardin P., *The Phenomenon of Man*, William Collins Sons & Co. Ltd., London 1959

The Subscription Economy Index, Subscribed Institute, March 2023, https://www.subscribedinstitute.com

Toffler A., *Future Shock*, Random House, New York 1970

United Nations Department of Economic and Social Affairs, Population Division (2019). World Population Prospects 2019: Highlights (ST/ESA/SER.A/423)

Vandermerwe S., Rada J., *Servitization of Business: Adding Value by Adding Services*, in European Management Journal, vol. 6, no 4, Winter 1988

Varian H.R. et al., *The Economics of Information Technology*, Cambridge University Press 2004

Wardley S., Wardley maps, Topographical intelligence in business; https://medium.com/wardleymaps/anticipation-89692e9b0ced

WEF Report, Industrial Internet of Things: Unleashing the Potential of Connected Products and Services, 2015 https://www3.weforum.org/docs/WEFUSA_IndustrialInternet_Re port2015.pdf

Weiser M., *The Computer for the 21st Century*, in Scientific American, Sept. 1991

Wheeler J.A., *The Outsider* in Newsweek, vol. 93, no. 11, Mar. 12, 1979

Wilson J.M., https://www.jackmwilson.net/Entrepreneurship/Cases/Moores-Meltcalfes-Gilders-Law.pdf

https://ec.europa.eu/info/research-and-innovation/research-area/industrial-research-and-innovation/industry-50_en

https://en.wikipedia.org/wiki/Cray-1

https://en.wikipedia.org/wiki/Gamification

https://en.wikipedia.org/wiki/List_of_rail_accidents_(2020%E2%8 0%93present)

https://insightmaker.com/insight/1954/The-World3-Model-Classic-World-Simulation

https://sustainabledevelopment.un.org/content/documents/5987our-common-future.pdf

https://www.bfi.org/about-fuller/big-ideas/dymaxion-world/dymaxion-house

https://www.bizjournals.com/sanjose/news/2019/04/23/tesla-robotaxis-owners-earn-money-musk-tsla.html

https://www.discovermagazine.com/technology/our-wonderful-age-of-abundance-in-9-striking-infographics

https://www.europarl.europa.eu/doceo/document/TA-9-2021-0040_EN.html

https://www.industryweek.com/leadership/companies-executives/article/21963777/driving-success-at-new-blue

https://www.informationisbeautiful.net/visualizations/million-lines-of-code/

https://www.keidanren.or.jp/en/policy/2016/029_outline.pdf

https://www.sae.org/news/press-room/2018/12/sae-international-releases-updated-visual-chart-for-its-%E2%80%9Clevels-of-driving-automation%E2%80%9D-standard-for-self-driving-vehicles

https://www.sciedupress.com/journal/index.php/jha/article/view/10752

https://www.technologyreview.com/2017/05/12/151722/nvidia-ceo-software-is-eating-the-world-but-ai-is-going-to-eat-software/

https://www.theinterline.com/06/2020/from-push-to-pull-how-technology-promises-to-reverse-the-flow-of-production/

https://www.un.org/sustainabledevelopment/blog/2018/05/68-of-the-world-population-projected-to-live-in-urban-areas-by-2050-says-un/

https://www.who.int/news-room/fact-sheets/detail/road-traffic-injuries

https://www.wsj.com/articles/SB10001424053111903480904576512250915629460

https://www8.cao.go.jp/cstp/kihonkeikaku/5basicplan_en.pdf

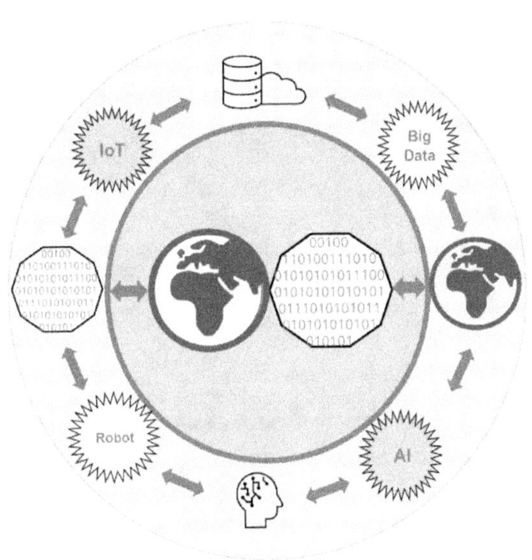

IoT
Big
Data
Robot
AI

www.ingramcontent.com/pod-product-compliance
Lightning Source LLC
Chambersburg PA
CBHW060046260726

48658CB00004B/1208